Project Management Institute

Combined
Standards
Glossary

Combined Standards Glossary

ISBN 13: 978-1-933890-27-2
ISBN 10: 1-93389-27-4

Published by: Project Management Institute, Inc.
                       Four Campus Boulevard
                       Newtown Square, Pennsylvania 19073-3299 USA.
                       Phone: +610-356-4600
                       Fax: +610-356-4647
                       E-mail: pmihq@pmi.org
                       Internet: www.pmi.org

PMI Publications welcomes corrections and comments on its books. Please feel free to send comments on typographical, formatting, or other errors. Simply make a copy of the relevant page of the book, mark the error, and send it to: Book Editor, PMI Publications, Four Campus Boulevard, Newtown Square, PA 19073-3299 USA.

PMI books are available at special quantity discounts to use as premiums and sales promotions, or for use in corporate training programs, as well as other educational programs. For more information, please write to Bookstore Administrator, PMI Publications, Four Campus Boulevard, Newtown Square, PA 19073-3299 USA, or e-mail: booksonline@pmi.org. Or contact your local bookstore.

10 9 8 7 6 5 4 3 2 1

TABLE OF CONTENTS

INTRODUCTION

The third edition of the *Combined Standards Glossary* interfiles in alphabetical order all glossary terms from the currently published PMI standards publications. The individual standards and their acronyms are:

- *A Guide to the Project Management Body of Knowledge (**PMBOK®** Guide* – **Third Edition)**
- Construction Extension to A Guide to the Project Management Body of Knowledge – 2000 Edition (***Const Ext***)
- *Government Extension to the PMBOK® Guide Third Edition (**Gov't Ext**)*
- Organizational Project Management Maturity Model (***OPM3®***)
- Practice Standard for Earned Value Management (***PS-EVM***)
- Practice Standard for Work Breakdown Structures – Second Edition (***PS-WBS***)
- Project Manager Competency Development (PMCD) Framework (***PMCDF***)
- The Standard for Portfolio Management (***Portfolio Management***)
- The Standard for Program Management (***Program Management***)

This edition of the *Combined Standards Glossary* is available for purchase by the general public as a print publication, and as a PDF document for PMI® members only. A special feature of the PDF version is the use of hyperlinks to connect terms with their definitions and show relationships between terms. Some glossary terms also include delimiting phrases in brackets (e.g., [Tool], [Process Group]), which are used to identify terms as Project Management Processes or Knowledge Areas, or to specify the functional relationship of terms to Project Management Processes.

This combined glossary includes acronyms and terms from current standards, practice standards, and extensions to the *PMBOK® Guide* that were published by December 2006. When discrepancies exist between a term's definitions in two or more standards, all definitions appear in the *Combined Standards Glossary*. (In such cases, definitions from the latest edition of the *PMBOK® Guide* are the preferred ones.)

Combined Standards Glossary
©2007 Project Management Institute, Four Campus Boulevard, Newtown Square, PA 19073-3299 USA

This publication is intended for use by both professionals and nonprofessionals interested in project management, including members and non-members of PMI, certified and non-certified project managers, writers, students, academicians, engineers, managers in a wide variety of industries, publishers, librarians, and members of the public. It remains a work in progress, growing and changing as the field of project management grows and changes. Comments and suggestions for improvement are welcome and should be sent to standards@pmi.org.

PMI® James R. Snyder Center for Project Management Knowledge & Wisdom,
PMI Publications Department, and PMI Standards Department
January 2007

COMMON ACRONYMS AND TERMS

Acronym	Term
AC	
	Actual Cost USE Actual Cost (AC) (*PMBOK® Guide* – **Third Edition**)
ACWP	
	Actual Cost of Work Performed (*PMBOK® Guide* – **Third Edition**) USE Actual Cost (AC) (*PMBOK® Guide* – **Third Edition**) **(*PS-WBS*)**
AD	
	Activity Description USE Activity Description (AD) (*PMBOK® Guide* – **Third Edition**)
ADM	
	Arrow Diagramming Method (*PMBOK® Guide* – **Third Edition**)
ADR	
	Alternative Dispute Resolution USE Alternative Dispute Resolution (ADR) (*Const Ext*)
AE	
	Apportioned Effort USE Apportioned Effort (AE) (*PMBOK® Guide* – **Third Edition**)(*PS-WBS*)
AF	
	Actual Finish Date USE Actual Finish Date (AF) (*PMBOK® Guide* – **Third Edition**)
AOA	
	Activity-on-Arrow (*PMBOK® Guide* – **Third Edition**) USE Arrow Diagramming Method (ACD) (*PMBOK® Guide* – **Third Edition**)
AON	
	Activity-on-Node (*PMBOK® Guide* – **Third Edition**) USE Precedence Diagramming Method (PDM) (*PMBOK® Guide* – **Third Edition**)
AS	
	Actual Start Date USE Actual Start Date (AS) (*PMBOK® Guide* – **Third Edition**)
BAC	
	Budget at Completion USE Budget at Completion (BAC) (*PMBOK® Guide* – **Third Edition**)

Combined Standards Glossary
©2007 Project Management Institute, Four Campus Boulevard, Newtown Square, PA 19073-3299 USA

BCWP

Budgeted Cost of Work Performed (*PMBOK® Guide* – **Third Edition**)
 USE Earned Value (EV) (*PMBOK® Guide* – **Third Edition**)

BCWS

Budgeted Cost of Work Scheduled (*PMBOK® Guide* – **Third Edition**)
 USE Planned Value (PV) (*PMBOK® Guide* – **Third Edition**)

BOM

Bill of Materials
 USE Bill of Materials (BOM) (*PMBOK® Guide* – **Third Edition**)

CA

Control Account
 USE Control Account (CA) (*PMBOK® Guide* – **Third Edition**)(*PS-WBS*)

CAP

Control Account Plan
 USE Control Account Plan (CAP) (*PMBOK® Guide* – **Third Edition**)

CCB

Change Control Board
 USE Change Control Board (CCB) (*PMBOK® Guide* – **Third Edition**)

COQ

Cost of Quality
 USE Cost of Quality (COQ) (*PMBOK® Guide* – **Third Edition**)

CPF

Cost-Plus-Fee
 USE Cost-Plus-Fee (CPF) (*PMBOK® Guide* – **Third Edition**)

CPFF

Cost-Plus-Fixed Fee
 USE Cost-Plus-Fixed-Fee (CPFF) Contract (*PMBOK® Guide* – **Third Edition**)

CPI

Cost Performance Index
 USE Cost Performance Index (CPI) (*PMBOK® Guide* – **Third Edition**)

CPIF

Cost-Plus-Incentive-Fee
 USE Cost-Plus-Incentive-Fee (CPIF) Contract (*PMBOK® Guide* – **Third Edition**)

Combined Standards Glossary

CPM

    Critical Path Method
      USE Critical Path Method (CPM) (*PMBOK® Guide* – **Third Edition**)

CPPC

    Cost-Plus-Percentage of Cost (*PMBOK® Guide* – **Third Edition**)
      USE Cost-Plus-Fee (CPF) (*PMBOK® Guide* – **Third Edition**)

CV

    Cost Variance
      USE Cost Variance (CV) (*PMBOK® Guide* – **Third Edition**)

CWBS

    Contract Work Breakdown Structure
      USE Contract Work Breakdown Structure (CWBS) (*PMBOK® Guide* – **Third Edition**)

DBOM

    Design-Build-Operate-Maintain
      USE Design-Build-Operate-Maintain (DBOM) (*Const Ext*)

DD

    Data Date
      USE Data Date (DD) (*PMBOK® Guide* – **Third Edition**)

DU

    Duration
      USE Duration (DU or DUR) (*PMBOK® Guide* – **Third Edition**)

DUR

    Duration
      USE Duration (DU or DUR) (*PMBOK® Guide* – **Third Edition**)

EAC

    Estimate at Completion
      USE Estimate at Completion (EAC) (*PMBOK® Guide* – **Third Edition**)

EF

    Early Finish Date
      USE Early Finish Date (EF) (*PMBOK® Guide* – **Third Edition**)

EMV

    Expected Monetary Value
      USE Expected Monetary Value (EMV) Analysis (*PMBOK® Guide* – **Third Edition**)

EPC

    Engineering-Procurement-Construction (*Const Ext*)

EPCM

    Engineering-Procurement-Construction Management (*Const Ext*)

Combined Standards Glossary
©2007 Project Management Institute, Four Campus Boulevard, Newtown Square, PA 19073-3299 USA

ES

Early Start Date
Use Early Start Date (ES) (***PMBOK® Guide* – Third Edition**)

ETC

Estimate to Complete
Use Estimate to Complete (ETC) (***PMBOK® Guide* – Third Edition**)

EV

Earned Value
Use Earned Value (EV) (***PMBOK® Guide* – Third Edition**)

EVM

Earned Value Management
Use Earned Value Management (EVM) (***PMBOK® Guide* – Third Edition**)

EVT

Earned Value Technique
Use Earned Value Technique (EVT) (***PMBOK® Guide* – Third Edition**)

FF

Finish-to-Finish
Use Finish-to-Finish (FF) (***PMBOK® Guide* – Third Edition**)

FF

Free Float
Use Free Float (FF) (***PMBOK® Guide* – Third Edition**)

FFP

Firm-Fixed-Price
Use Firm-Fixed-Price (FFP) Contract (***PMBOK® Guide* – Third Edition**)

FMEA

Failure Mode and Effect Analysis
Use Failure Mode and Effect Analysis (FMEA) (***PMBOK® Guide* – Third Edition**)

FPIF

Fixed-Price-Incentive-Fee
Use Fixed-Price-Incentive-Fee (FPIF) Contract (***PMBOK® Guide* – Third Edition**)

FS

Finish-to-Start
Use Finish-to-Start (FS) (***PMBOK® Guide* – Third Edition**)

IDIQ

Indefinite Delivery Indefinite Quantity Contracts
Use Indefinite Delivery Indefinite Quantity Contracts (IDIQ) (***Gov't Ext***)

Acronym   Term

IFB

Invitation for Bid
Use Invitation for Bid (IFB) (*PMBOK® Guide – Third Edition*)

IPECC

The Initiating, Planning, Executing, Monitoring and Controlling, and Closing Process Groups (*Program Management*)
Use Indefinite Delivery Indefinite Quantity Contracts (IDIQ) (*Gov't Ext*)

LF

Late Finish Date
Use Late Finish Date (LF) (*PMBOK® Guide – Third Edition*)

LOE

Level of Effort
Use Level of Effort (LOE) (*PMBOK® Guide – Third Edition*)(*PS-WBS*)

LS

Late Start Date
Use Late Start Date (LS) (*PMBOK® Guide – Third Edition*)

OBS

Organizational Breakdown Structure
Use Organizational Breakdown Structure (OBS) (*PMBOK® Guide – Third Edition*)(*PS-WBS*)

OD

Original Duration
Use Original Duration (OD) (*PMBOK® Guide – Third Edition*)

OPM

Organizational Project Management
Use Organizational Project Management (OPM) (*OPM3*)

OPM3®

Organizational Project Management Maturity Model (*OPM3*)

PC

Percent Complete
Use Percent Complete (PC or PCT) (*PMBOK® Guide – Third Edition*)

PCT

Percent Complete
Use Percent Complete (PC or PCT) (*PMBOK® Guide – Third Edition*)

PDA

Personal Data Assistant
Use Personal Data Assistant (PDA) (*Const Ext*)

PDM

Precedence Diagramming Method
Use Precedence Diagramming Method (PDM) (*PMBOK® Guide –* **Third Edition)**

PF

Planned Finish Date (*PMBOK® Guide –* **Third Edition)**
Use Scheduled Finish Date (SF) (*PMBOK® Guide –* **Third Edition)**

PM

Project Management
Use Project Management (PM) (*PMBOK® Guide –* **Third Edition)**

PM

Project Manager
Use Project Manager (PM) (*PMBOK® Guide –* **Third Edition)**

PMB

Performance Measurement Baseline
Use Performance Measurement Baseline (PMB) (*PMBOK® Guide –* **Third Edition)**

PMBOK

Project Management Body of Knowledge
Use Project Management Body of Knowledge (*PMBOK® Guide –* **Third Edition)(*Program Management*)**

PMIS

Project Management Information System
Use Project Management Information System (PMIS) (*PMBOK® Guide –* **Third Edition)**

PMO

Program Management Office
Use Program Management Office (PMO) (*PMBOK® Guide –* **Third Edition)(*Program Management*)**

PMO

Project Management Office
Use Project Management Office (PMO) (*PMBOK® Guide –* **Third Edition)(*Program Management*)**

PMP®

Project Management Professional
Use Project Management Professional (PMP®) (*PMBOK®* **Guide – Third Edition)**

PPP

Project, Program, and Portfolio Management (*OPM3*)

PS

Planned Start Date (*PMBOK® Guide –* **Third Edition)**
Use Scheduled Start Date (SS) (*PMBOK® Guide –* **Third Edition)**

Combined Standards Glossary

Acronym	Term

PSWBS

Project Summary Work Breakdown Structure
Use Project Summary Work Breakdown Structure (PSWBS) *(PMBOK® Guide – Third Edition)*

PV

Planned Value
Use Planned Value (PV) *(PMBOK® Guide – Third Edition)*

QA

Quality Assurance *(PMBOK® Guide – Third Edition)*

QC

Quality Control *(PMBOK® Guide – Third Edition)*

RAM

Responsibility Assignment Matrix
Use Responsibility Assignment Matrix (RAM) *(PMBOK® Guide – Third Edition) (PS-WBS)*

RBS

Resource Breakdown Structure
Use Resource Breakdown Structure (RBS) *(PMBOK® Guide – Third Edition) (PS-WBS)*

RBS

Risk Breakdown Structure
Use Risk Breakdown Structure (RBS) *(PMBOK® Guide – Third Edition)(PS-WBS)*

RD

Remaining Duration
Use Remaining Duration (RD) *(PMBOK® Guide – Third Edition)*

RFI

Request for Information
Use Request for Information (RFI) *(PMBOK® Guide – Third Edition)*

RFP

Request for Proposal
Use Request for Proposal (RFP) *(PMBOK® Guide – Third Edition)*

RFQ

Request for Quotation
Use Request for Quotation (RFQ) *(PMBOK® Guide – Third Edition)*

SF

Scheduled Finish Date
Use Scheduled Finish Date (SF) *(PMBOK® Guide – Third Edition)*

Combined Standards Glossary
©2007 Project Management Institute, Four Campus Boulevard, Newtown Square, PA 19073-3299 USA

SF

Start-to-Finish
Use Start-to-Finish (SF) (*PMBOK® Guide* – **Third Edition**)

SMCI

Standardize, Measure, Control, Improve
Use SMCI *(OPM3)*

SOW

Statement of Work
Use Statement of Work (SOW) (*PMBOK® Guide* – **Third Edition**) (*PS-WBS*)

SPI

Schedule Performance Index
Use Schedule Performance Index (SPI) (*PMBOK® Guide* – **Third Edition**)

SS

Scheduled Start Date
Use Scheduled Start Date (SS) (*PMBOK® Guide* – **Third Edition**)

SS

Start-to-Start
Use Start-to-Start (SS) (*PMBOK® Guide* – **Third Edition**)

SV

Schedule Variance
Use Schedule Variance (SV) (*PMBOK® Guide* – **Third Edition**)

SWOT

Strengths, Weaknesses, Opportunities, and Threats
Use Strengths, Weaknesses, Opportunities, and Threats (SWOT) (*PMBOK® Guide* – **Third Edition**)

T&M

Time and Material
Use Time and Material (T&M) Contract (*PMBOK® Guide* – **Third Edition**)

TC

Target Completion Date
Use Target Completion Date (TC) (*PMBOK® Guide* – **Third Edition**)

TCPI

To-Complete Performance Index
Use To-Complete Performance Index (TCPI) (*PS-EVM*)

TF

Target Finish Date
Use Target Finish Date (TF) (*PMBOK® Guide* – **Third Edition**)

Combined Standards Glossary
©2007 Project Management Institute, Four Campus Boulevard, Newtown Square, PA 19073-3299 USA

TF

Total Float
Use Total Float (TF) (*PMBOK® Guide – Third Edition*)

TQM

Total Quality Management
Use Total Quality Management (TQM) (*PMBOK® Guide – Third Edition*)

TS

Target Start Date
Use Target Start Date (TS) (*PMBOK® Guide – Third Edition*)

VAC

Variance at Completion
Use Variance at Completion (VAC) (*PS-EVM*)

VE

Value Engineering
Use Value Engineering (VE) (*PMBOK® Guide – Third Edition*)

WBS

Work Breakdown Structure
Use
Work Breakdown Structure (WBS) (*PMBOK® Guide – Third Edition*)(*PS-WBS*)

TERMS AND DEFINITIONS

Ability

The quality of being able to do something; the physical, mental, financial, or legal power to perform; a natural or acquired skill or talent. (*PMCDF*)

Accept

The act of formally receiving or acknowledging something and regarding it as being true, sound, suitable, or complete. (*PMBOK® Guide* – **Third Edition**)

Acceptance

SEE *Accept* (*PMBOK® Guide* – **Third Edition**)

Acceptance Criteria

Those criteria, including performance requirements and essential conditions, which must be met before project deliverables are accepted. (*PMBOK® Guide* – **Third Edition**)

ACCPAC (International, Inc.)

A business services and application software firm providing accounting software among other products. (*Const Ext*)

Acquire Project Team [Process]

The process of obtaining the human resources needed to complete the project. (*PMBOK® Guide* – **Third Edition**)

Activity

A component of work performed during the course of a project. (*PMBOK® Guide* – **Third Edition**)(*PS-WBS*)

SEE ALSO Schedule Activity
(*PMBOK® Guide* – **Third Edition**)

Activity Attributes [Output/Input]

Multiple attributes associated with each *schedule activity* that can be included within the activity list. Activity attributes include activity codes, predecessor activities, successor activities, logical relationships, leads and lags, resource requirements, imposed dates, constraints, and assumptions. (*PMBOK® Guide* – **Third Edition**)

Combined Standards Glossary
©2007 Project Management Institute, Four Campus Boulevard, Newtown Square, PA 19073-3299 USA

Activity Code

One or more numerical or text values that identify characteristics of the work or in some way categorize the schedule activity that allows filtering and ordering of activities within reports. (*PMBOK® Guide* – **Third Edition**)

Activity Definition [Process]

The process of identifying the specific schedule activities that need to be performed to produce the various project deliverables. (*PMBOK® Guide* – **Third Edition**)

Activity Description (AD)

A short phrase or label for each schedule activity used in conjunction with an activity identifier to differentiate that project schedule activity from other schedule activities. The activity description normally describes the scope of work of the schedule activity. (*PMBOK® Guide* – **Third Edition**)

Activity Duration

The time in calendar units between the start and finish of a schedule activity. (*PMBOK® Guide* – **Third Edition**)

> SEE ALSO   Actual Duration
> (*PMBOK® Guide* – **Third Edition**)
> Original Duration (OD)
> (*PMBOK® Guide* – **Third Edition**)
> Remaining Duration (RD)
> (*PMBOK® Guide* – **Third Edition**)

Activity Duration Estimating [Process]

The process of estimating the number of work periods that will be needed to complete individual schedule activities. (*PMBOK® Guide* – **Third Edition**)

Activity Identifier

A short unique numeric or text identification assigned to each schedule activity to differentiate that project activity from other activities. Typically unique within any one project schedule network diagram. (*PMBOK® Guide* – **Third Edition**)

Activity List [Output/Input]

A documented tabulation of schedule activities that shows the activity description, activity identifier, and a sufficiently detailed scope of work description so project team members understand what work is to be performed. (*PMBOK® Guide* – **Third Edition**)

Combined Standards Glossary
©2007 Project Management Institute, Four Campus Boulevard, Newtown Square, PA 19073-3299 USA

Activity-on-Arrow (AOA)

SEE   Arrow Diagramming Method (ADM)
       (*PMBOK® Guide* – **Third Edition**)

Activity-on-Node (AON)

SEE   Precedence Diagramming Method (PDM)
       (*PMBOK® Guide* – **Third Edition**)

Activity Resource Estimating [Process]

The process of estimating the types and quantities of resources required to perform each schedule activity. (*PMBOK® Guide* – **Third Edition**)

Activity Sequencing [Process]

The process of identifying and documenting dependencies among schedule activities. (*PMBOK® Guide* – **Third Edition**)

Actual Cost (AC)

1) Total costs actually incurred and recorded in accomplishing work performed for a schedule activity or work breakdown structure component. Actual cost can sometimes be direct labor hours alone, direct costs alone, or all costs including indirect costs. Also referred to as the actual cost of work performed (ACWP). (*PMBOK® Guide* – **Third Edition**)

2) Total costs actually incurred and recorded in accomplishing work performed during a given time period. (Note: The *PMBOK® Guide* – Third Edition definition for this term is broader and more inclusive in that it applies beyond the scope of the *Practice Standard for Earned Value Management*.) (*PS-EVM*)

    SEE ALSO   Earned Value Management (EVM)
                (*PMBOK® Guide* – **Third Edition**)
                Earned Value Technique (EVT)
                (*PMBOK® Guide* – **Third Edition**)

Actual Cost of Work Performed (ACWP)

SEE   Actual Cost (AC)
       (*PMBOK® Guide* – **Third Edition**) (*PS-EVM*)

Actual Duration

The time in calendar units between the actual start date of the schedule activity and either the data date of the project schedule if the schedule activity is in progress or the actual finish date if the schedule activity is complete. (*PMBOK® Guide* – **Third Edition**)

Actual Finish Date (AF)

The point in time that work actually ended on a schedule activity. (Note: In some application areas, the schedule activity is considered "finished" when work is "substantially complete.") (*PMBOK® Guide* – **Third Edition**)

Actual Start Date (AS)

The point in time that work actually started on a schedule activity. (*PMBOK® Guide* – **Third Edition**)

Advertisement

A formal notice of a government contracting opportunity intended to ensure full and open competition. The notice is typically published in a newspaper of general circulation and/or publications of professional societies, as well as contract registers of government bodies. (*Gov't Ext*)

Alternative Dispute Resolution (ADR)

Methods, other than litigation, for resolving disputes, including arbitration, mediation and mini-trials. (*Const Ext*)

Analogous Estimating [Technique]

An estimating technique that uses the values of parameters, such as scope, cost, budget, and duration or measures of scale such as size, weight, and complexity from a previous, similar activity as the basis for estimating the same parameter or measure for a future activity. It is frequently used to estimate a parameter when there is a limited amount of detailed information about the project (e.g., in the early phases). Analogous estimating is a form of expert judgment. Analogous estimating is most reliable when the previous activities are similar in fact and not just in appearance, and the project team members preparing the estimates have the needed expertise. (*PMBOK® Guide* – **Third Edition**)

Application Area

A category of projects that have common components significant in such projects, but are not needed or present in all projects. Application areas are usually defined in terms of either the product (i.e., by similar technologies or production methods) or the type of customer (i.e., internal versus external, government versus commercial) or industry sector (i.e., utilities, automotive, aerospace, information technologies). Application areas can overlap. (*PMBOK® Guide* – **Third Edition**)

Apportioned Effort (AE)

Effort applied to project work that is not readily divisible into discrete efforts for that work, but which is related in direct proportion to measurable discrete work efforts. Contrast with *discrete effort.* (*PMBOK® Guide* – **Third Edition**) (*PS-EVM*)(*PS-WBS*)

Combined Standards Glossary
©2007 Project Management Institute, Four Campus Boulevard, Newtown Square, PA 19073-3299 USA

Appropriation

An action by a government body to provide funding for a line item project or a program. Appropriations are typically contained in the budget of the governmental body, but may also be enacted separately. See also *Line Item Projects* and *Program*. (*Gov't Ext*)

SEE ALSO   *Line Item Projects* and *Program* (*Gov't Ext*)

Approval

SEE   Approve (*PMBOK® Guide* – **Third Edition**)

Approve

The act of formally confirming, sanctioning, ratifying, or agreeing to something. (*PMBOK® Guide* – **Third Edition**)

Approved Change Request [Output/Input]

A change request that has been processed through the integrated change control process and approved. Contrast with *requested change*. (*PMBOK® Guide* – **Third Edition**)

Arrow

The graphic presentation of a schedule activity in the arrow diagramming method or a logical relationship between schedule activities in the precedence diagramming method. (*PMBOK® Guide* – **Third Edition**)

Arrow Diagramming Method (ADM) [Technique]

A schedule network diagramming technique in which schedule activities are represented by arrows. The tail of the arrow represents the start, and the head represents the finish of the schedule activity. (The length of the arrow does **not** represent the expected duration of the schedule activity.) Schedule activities are connected at points called nodes (usually drawn as small circles) to illustrate the sequence in which the schedule activities are expected to be performed. (*PMBOK® Guide* – **Third Edition**)

SEE ALSO   Precedence Diagramming Method (PDM) (*PMBOK® Guide* – **Third Edition**)

As-of Date

SEE   Data Date (DD) (*PMBOK® Guide* – **Third Edition**)

Assumptions [Output/Input]

Assumptions are factors that, for planning purposes, are considered to be true, real, or certain without proof or demonstration. Assumptions affect all aspects of project planning, and are part of the progressive elaboration of the project. Project teams frequently identify, document, and validate assumptions as part of their planning process. Assumptions generally involve a degree of risk. (*PMBOK® Guide* – **Third Edition**)

Combined Standards Glossary
©2007 Project Management Institute, Four Campus Boulevard, Newtown Square, PA 19073-3299 USA

Assumptions Analysis [Technique]

A technique that explores the accuracy of assumptions and identifies risks to the project from inaccuracy, inconsistency, or incompleteness of assumptions. (*PMBOK® Guide* – **Third Edition**)

Attitudes

Relatively lasting feelings, beliefs, and behavior tendencies directed toward specific persons, groups, ideas, issues, or objects. They are often described in terms of three components: 1) an affective component, or the feelings, sentiments, moods, and emotions about some person, idea, event, or object; 2) a cognitive component, or the beliefs, opinions, knowledge, or information held by the individual; and 3) a behavioral component, or the intention and predisposition to act. (*PMCDF*)

Authority

The right to apply project resources, expend funds, make decisions, or give approvals. (*PMBOK® Guide* – **Third Edition**)

Authorization

The process of approving, funding, and communicating the authorization for initiating work on a component included in the "balanced portfolio." (*Portfolio Management*)

Backward Pass

The calculation of late finish dates and late start dates for the uncompleted portions of all schedule activities. Determined by working backwards through the schedule network logic from the project's end date. The end date may be calculated in a forward pass or set by the customer or sponsor. (*PMBOK® Guide* – **Third Edition**)

        SEE ALSO   Schedule Network Analysis
                         (*PMBOK® Guide* – **Third Edition**)

Bar Chart [Tool]

A graphic display of schedule-related information. In the typical bar chart, schedule activities or work breakdown structure components are listed down the left side of the chart, dates are shown across the top, and activity durations are shown as date-placed horizontal bars. Also called a Gantt chart. (*PMBOK® Guide* – **Third Edition**)

Baseline

The approved time phased plan (for a project, a work breakdown structure component, a work package, or a schedule activity), plus or minus approved project scope, cost, schedule, and technical changes. Generally refers to the current baseline, but may refer to the original or some other baseline. Usually used with a modifier (e.g., cost baseline,

Combined Standards Glossary
©2007 Project Management Institute, Four Campus Boulevard, Newtown Square, PA 19073-3299 USA

schedule baseline, performance measurement baseline, technical baseline). (*PMBOK® Guide* – **Third Edition**)

SEE ALSO   Performance Measurement Baseline (PMB)
(*PMBOK® Guide* – **Third Edition**)

Baseline Finish Date

The finish date of a schedule activity in the approved schedule baseline. (*PMBOK® Guide* – **Third Edition**)

SEE ALSO   Scheduled Finish Date (SF)
(*PMBOK® Guide* – **Third Edition**)

Baseline Start Date

The start date of a schedule activity in the approved schedule baseline. (*PMBOK® Guide* – **Third Edition**)

SEE ALSO   Scheduled Start Date (SS)
(*PMBOK® Guide* – **Third Edition**)

Behavior

The manner in which an individual acts or conducts oneself under specified circumstances. (*PMCDF*)

Benefit

An improvement to the running of an organization such as increased sales, reduced running costs, or reduced waste. (*Program Management*)

Benefits Management

Activities and techniques for defining, creating, maximizing, and sustaining the benefits provided by programs. (*Program Management*)

Benefits Realization Plan

A document detailing the expected benefits to be realized by a program and how these benefits will be achieved. (*Program Management*)

Best Practice

A Best Practice is an optimal way currently recognized by industry to achieve a stated goal or objective. For organizational project management, this includes the ability to deliver projects successfully, consistently, and predictably to implement organizational strategies. (*OPM3*)

Best Practices Directory

The Best Practices Directory lists the nearly 600 Best Practices that form the foundation of OPM3. This Directory provides the name and a brief description of each Best Practice. By reviewing the Best Practices Directory, the user can become generally familiar with the OPM3 content. An organization will also use this Directory following the Self-Assessment to identify Best Practices for any potential improvement effort.

Combined Standards Glossary
©2007 Project Management Institute, Four Campus Boulevard, Newtown Square, PA 19073-3299 USA

The Best Practices Directory appears in an appendix to the *OPM3*. It identifies each Best Practice, and indicates to which of the three Domains the Best Practice applies (Project, Program or Portfolio), as well as to which of the four stages of process improvement (Standardize, Measure, Control, Improve) the Best Practice applies. (***OPM3***)

Best Value Selection

A selection process in which proposals submitted by potential sellers are evaluated using several factors including the seller's price. Each seller receives a quantitative point score for each factor except for price, which is already quantified. The process often involves assigning a predetermined weight to each factor; however, a government body may elect not to assign a weight to price. If a weight is assigned to price, a contract is awarded to the seller with the best weighted score. If a weight is not assigned to price, each seller's price can be divided by the weighted score of other factors and the contract awarded to the seller with the lowest price per point. Alternatively, the selection process may perform an evaluation of sellers and determine which proposal is most advantageous to the government body without use of weights to combine factors. (***Gov't Ext***)

Bill of Materials (BOM)

A documented formal hierarchical tabulation of the physical assemblies, subassemblies, and components needed to fabricate a product. (***PMBOK®** Guide* – **Third Edition**)

Bottom-up Estimating [Technique]

A method of estimating a component of work. The work is decomposed into more detail. An estimate is prepared of what is needed to meet the requirements of each of the lower, more detailed pieces of work, and these estimates are then aggregated into a total quantity for the component of work. The accuracy of bottom-up estimating is driven by the size and complexity of the work identified at the lower levels. Generally smaller work scopes increase the accuracy of the estimates. (***PMBOK®** Guide* – **Third Edition**)

Brainstorming [Technique]

A general data gathering and creativity technique that can be used to identify risks, ideas, or solutions to issues by using a group of team members or subject-matter experts. Typically, a brainstorming session is structured so that each participant's ideas are recorded for later analysis. (***PMBOK®** Guide* – **Third Edition**)

Budget

The approved estimate for the project or any work breakdown structure component or any schedule activity. (*PMBOK® Guide* – **Third Edition**)

  SEE ALSO   Estimate (*PMBOK® Guide* – **Third Edition**)

Budget at Completion (BAC)

1) The sum of all the *budgets* established for the *work* to be performed on a *project* or a *work breakdown structure component* or a *schedule activity*. The total *planned value* for the project. (*PMBOK® Guide* – **Third Edition**)

2) The sum of all the budgets established for the work to be performed on the project. The total planned value for the project. (Note: The *PMBOK® Guide* – Third Edition definition for this term is broader and more inclusive in that it applies beyond the scope of the *Practice Standard for Earned Value Management*.) (*PS-EVM*)

Budgeted Cost of Work Performed (BCWP)

SEE   Earned Value (EV)
      (*PMBOK® Guide* – **Third Edition**) (*PS-EVM*)

Budgeted Cost of Work Scheduled (BCWS)

SEE   Planned Value (PV)
      (*PMBOK® Guide* – **Third Edition**) (*PS-EVM*)

Buffer

SEE   Reserve (*PMBOK® Guide* – **Third Edition**)

Business Case

A documented economic feasibility study used to establish validity of the benefits of a selected component lacking sufficient definition and that is used as a basis for the authorization of further project management activities. (*Portfolio Management*)

Business Outcome

A financial result (cost saving, opportunity, employee reduction, revenue growth, revenue retention) derived from implementing an organization's strategies. (*Portfolio Management*)

Buyer

The acquirer of products, services, or results for an organization. (*PMBOK® Guide* – **Third Edition**)

Combined Standards Glossary
©2007 Project Management Institute, Four Campus Boulevard, Newtown Square, PA 19073-3299 USA

Calendar Unit

The smallest unit of time used in scheduling the project. Calendar units are generally in hours, days, or weeks, but can also be in quarter years, months, shifts, or even in minutes. (*PMBOK® Guide* – **Third Edition**)

Capabilities Directory

The Capabilities Directory provides detailed data on each of the Capabilities, organized according to the Best Practices with which they are associated. The Capabilities Directory is central to the second Assessment step, in which the user is able to determine which Capabilities currently exist in the organization and which do not.

The Capabilities Directory appears in an appendix to the *OPM3*. For each Best Practice, it includes a list of its constituent Capabilities, including their associated Outcomes, Key Performance Indicators and Metrics that should be confirmed to claim the existence of this Capability.

Each Capability contains an ID number, the domain(s) (Project, Program, or Portfolio), Process Improvement Stage(s) (Standardize, Measure, Control, or Improve) and the *PMBOK® Guide* Process Group(s) (Initiate, Plan, Execute, Control, or Closeout) to which the Capability applies. (*OPM3*)

Capability

A Capability is a specific competency that must exist in an organization in order for it to execute project management processes and deliver project management services and products. Capabilities are incremental steps leading up to one or more Best Practices. (*OPM3*)

Capacity

The resources (human resources, financial, physical assets) which an organization puts at the disposal of portfolio management to select, fund, and execute its components. (*Portfolio Management*)

Categorization

The process of grouping potential components into categories to facilitate further decision-making. (*Portfolio Management*)

Categorization/Mapping

Categorizations are groupings to provide structure and a framework for OPM3 so that the relationship between Best Practices and Capabilities could be better understood. It also allows organizations to focus on alternative approaches to maturity.

The three categorizations in the model are PPP (Portfolio, Program, or Project), SMCI (Standardize, Measure, Control, or Improve), and IPECC (Initiate, Plan, Execute, Control, and Close). These categorizations can be used to approach OPM3 from a project management domain, an improvement process, or a process area, respectively. As such, each Best Practice and Capability is mapped to one category in each of the above three categorizations.

SEE ALSO   Domain, PPP, and SMCI in this Glossary for more details. (*OPM3*)

Category

A predetermined key description used to group potential and authorized components to facilitate further decision-making. Categories usually link their components with a common set of strategic goals. (*Portfolio Management*)

Change Control

Identifying, documenting, approving or rejecting, and controlling changes to the project baseline. (*PMBOK® Guide* – **Third Edition**)

Change Control Board (CCB)

A formally constituted group of stakeholders responsible for reviewing, evaluating, approving, delaying, or rejecting changes to the project, with all decisions and recommendations being recorded. (*PMBOK® Guide* – **Third Edition**)

Change Control System [Tool]

A collection of formal documented procedures that define how project deliverables and documentation will be controlled, changed, and approved. In most application areas the change control system is a subset of the configuration management system. (*PMBOK® Guide* – **Third Edition**)

Change Request

Requests to expand or reduce the project scope, modify policies, processes, plans, or procedures, modify costs or budgets, or revise schedules. Requests for a change can be direct or indirect, externally or internally initiated, and legally or contractually mandated or optional. Only formally documented requested changes are processed and only approved change requests are implemented. (*PMBOK® Guide* – **Third Edition**)

Chart of Accounts [Tool]

Any numbering system used to monitor project costs by category (e.g., labor, supplies, materials, and equipment). The project chart of accounts is usually based upon the corporate chart of accounts of the primary performing organization. Contrast with *code of accounts*. (*PMBOK® Guide* – **Third Edition**)

Combined Standards Glossary
©2007 Project Management Institute, Four Campus Boulevard, Newtown Square, PA 19073-3299 USA

Charter

SEE Project Charter (*PMBOK® Guide* – **Third Edition**)

Checklist [Output/Input]

Items listed together for convenience of comparison, or to ensure the actions associated with them are managed appropriately and not forgotten. An example is a list of items to be inspected that is created during quality planning and applied during quality control. (***PMBOK® Guide* – Third Edition**)

Civil Service System

A system in which government employees hold office from one administration to another. Their positions are protected provided that they remain politically neutral. (***Gov't Ext***)

SEE ALSO Spoils System (***Gov't Ext***)

Claim

A request, demand, or assertion of rights by a seller against a buyer, or vice versa, for consideration, compensation, or payment under the terms of a legally binding contract, such as for a disputed change. (***PMBOK® Guide* – Third Edition**)

Class

A key descriptor telling if a (potential) component is a business case, a project, a program, a portfolio or other work. (***Portfolio Management***)

Close Project [Process]

The process of finalizing all activities across all of the project process groups to formally close the project or phase. (***PMBOK® Guide* – Third Edition**)

Closing Processes [Process Group]

1) Those processes performed to formally terminate all activities of a project or phase, and transfer the completed product to others or close a cancelled project. (***PMBOK® Guide* – Third Edition**)

2) Those processes performed to formally terminate all activities of a program or phase, and transfer the completed product to others or close a cancelled program. (***Program Management***)

Code of Accounts [Tool]

Any numbering system used to uniquely identify each component of the work breakdown structure. Contrast with *chart of accounts*. (***PMBOK® Guide* – Third Edition**)

Combined Standards Glossary
©2007 Project Management Institute, Four Campus Boulevard, Newtown Square, PA 19073-3299 USA

Co-location [Technique]

An organizational placement strategy where the project team members are physically located close to one another in order to improve communication, working relationships, and productivity. (*PMBOK® Guide* – **Third Edition**)

Common Cause

A source of variation that is inherent in the system and predictable. On a control chart, it appears as part of the random process variation (i.e., variation from a process that would be considered normal or not unusual), and is indicated by a random pattern of points within the control limits. Also referred to as random cause. Contrast with *special cause*. (*PMBOK® Guide* – **Third Edition**)

Communication

A process through which information is exchanged among persons using a common system of symbols, signs, or behaviors. (*PMBOK® Guide* – **Third Edition**)

Communication Management Plan [Output/Input]

The document that describes: the communications needs and expectations for the project; how and in what format information will be communicated; when and where each communication will be made; and who is responsible for providing each type of communication. A communication management plan can be formal or informal, highly detailed or broadly framed, based on the requirements of the project stakeholders. The communication management plan is contained in, or is a subsidiary plan of, the project management plan. (*PMBOK® Guide* – **Third Edition**)

Communications Planning [Process]

The process of determining the information and communications needs of the project stakeholders: who they are, what is their level of interest and influence on the project, who needs what information, when will they need it, and how it will be given to them. (*PMBOK® Guide* – **Third Edition**)

Compensation

Something given or received, a payment or recompense, usually something monetary or in kind for products, services, or results provided or received. (*PMBOK® Guide* – **Third Edition**)

©2007 Project Management Institute, Four Campus Boulevard, Newtown Square, PA 19073-3299 USA

Competency

A cluster of related knowledge, attitudes, skills, and other personal characteristics that affects a major part of one's job (i.e., one or more key roles or responsibilities), correlates with performance on the job, can be measured against well-accepted standards, and can be improved via training and development.

Major components of competencies include:

- Abilities
- Attitudes
- Behavior
- Knowledge
- Personality
- Skills

Major dimensions of competency include:

PM Knowledge Competency: The knowledge and understanding that a project manager brings to a project. This can include qualifications and experience, both direct and related. These are the knowledge components of competence.

Personal Competency: The core personality characteristics underlying a person's capability to do a project. These are the behavior, motives, traits, attitudes, and self-concepts that enable a person to successfully manage a project.

PM Performance Competency: The ability to perform the activities within an occupational area to the levels of performance expected in employment. This competency dimension looks at the demonstrable performance of the individual in executing project management tasks. (*PMCDF*)

Competency Cluster

SEE   Competency (*PMCDF*)

Competency Dictionary

A general comprehensive list of the competencies that are included in the competency framework for a job, usually grouped by clusters. (*PMCDF*)

Competency Dimensions

A multidimensional framework that breaks competency into dimensions of knowledge, performance and personal competence. (*PMCDF*)

Combined Standards Glossary
©2007 Project Management Institute, Four Campus Boulevard, Newtown Square, PA 19073-3299 USA

Competency Gap

The difference between the desired level of competence within a given dimension and the level of competence assessed for an individual. It is the "gaps" in one's competence that an individual aims to improve through individual development. (*PMCDF*)

Component

1) A constituent part, element, or piece of a complex whole. (PMBOK® Guide – Third Edition)
2) An activity or set of activities which is managed using the project portfolio management process, namely a business case, a project, a program, a portfolio, or other work that fits into the "component definition" used by an organization. (*Portfolio Management*)

Configuration Management System [Tool]

A subsystem of the overall project management system. It is a collection of formal documented procedures used to apply technical and administrative direction and surveillance to: identify and document the functional and physical characteristics of a product, result, service, or component; control any changes to such characteristics; record and report each change and its implementation status; and support the audit of the products, results, or components to verify conformance to requirements. It includes the documentation, tracking systems, and defined approval levels necessary for authorizing and controlling changes. In most application areas, the configuration management system includes the change control system. (*PMBOK® Guide* – **Third Edition**)

Consortium

Similar to a joint venture, a group of companies formed to undertake a project beyond the resources of any one member. (***Const Ext***)

Constraint [Input]

The state, quality, or sense of being restricted to a given course of action or inaction. An applicable restriction or limitation, either internal or external to the project, that will affect the performance of the project or a process. For example, a schedule constraint is any limitation or restraint placed on the project schedule that affects when a schedule activity can be scheduled and is usually in the form of fixed imposed dates. A cost constraint is any limitation or restraint placed on the project budget such as funds available over time. A project resource constraint is any limitation or restraint placed on resource usage, such as what resource skills or disciplines are available and the amount of a given resource available during a specified time frame. (*PMBOK® Guide* – **Third Edition**)

Combined Standards Glossary
©2007 Project Management Institute, Four Campus Boulevard, Newtown Square, PA 19073-3299 USA

Constructability

The ease, safety, economy and clarity of construction of a project. (***Const Ext***)

Contingency

SEE   Reserve (***PMBOK® Guide* – Third Edition**)

Contingency Allowance

SEE   Reserve (***PMBOK® Guide* – Third Edition**)

Contingency Reserve [Output/Input]

The amount of funds, budget, or time needed above the estimate to reduce the risk of overruns of project objectives to a level acceptable to the organization. (***PMBOK® Guide* – Third Edition**)

Contract [Output/Input]

A contract is a mutually binding agreement that obligates the seller to provide the specified product or service or result and obligates the buyer to pay for it. (***PMBOK® Guide* – Third Edition**)

Contract Administration [Process]

The process of managing the contract and the relationship between the buyer and seller, reviewing and documenting how a seller is performing or has performed to establish required corrective actions and provide a basis for future relationships with the seller, managing contract related changes and, when appropriate, managing the contractual relationship with the outside buyer of the project. (***PMBOK® Guide* – Third Edition**)

Contract Closure [Process]

The process of completing and settling the contract, including resolution of any open items and closing each contract. (***PMBOK® Guide* – Third Edition**)

Contract Management Plan [Output/Input]

The document that describes how a specific contract will be administered and can include items such as required documentation delivery and performance requirements. A contract management plan can be formal or informal, highly detailed or broadly framed, based on the requirements in the contract. Each contract management plan is a subsidiary plan of the project management plan. (***PMBOK® Guide* – Third Edition**)

Contract Statement of Work (SOW) [Output/Input]

A narrative description of products, services, or results to be supplied under contract. (***PMBOK® Guide* – Third Edition**)

Combined Standards Glossary
©2007 Project Management Institute, Four Campus Boulevard, Newtown Square, PA 19073-3299 USA

Contract Work Breakdown Structure (CWBS) [Output/Input]

A portion of the work breakdown structure for the project developed and maintained by a seller contracting to provide a subproject or project component. (*PMBOK® Guide* – **Third Edition**)

Control [Technique]

Comparing actual performance with planned performance, analyzing variances, assessing trends to effect process improvements, evaluating possible alternatives, and recommending appropriate corrective action as needed. (*PMBOK® Guide* – **Third Edition**)(*Program Management*)

Control Account (CA) [Tool]

1) A management control point where *scope*, *budget* (resource plans), *actual cost*, and *schedule* are integrated and compared to *earned value* for performance measurement. Control accounts are placed at selected management points (specific *components* at selected levels) of the *work breakdown structure*. Each control account may include one or more *work packages*, but each work package may be associated with only one control account. Each control account is associated with a specific single organizational *component* in the *organizational breakdown structure* (OBS). Previously called a Cost Account. (*PMBOK® Guide* – **Third Edition**)(*PS-WBS*)

2) A management control point where scope, budget (resource plans), actual cost, and schedule are integrated and compared to earned value for performance measurement. Control accounts are placed at selected management points (specific components at selected levels) of the work breakdown structure. (Note: The *PMBOK® Guide* – Third Edition definition for this term is broader and more inclusive in that it applies beyond the scope of the *Practice Standard for Earned Value Management*.) (*PS-EVM*)

> See Also   Work Package
> (*PMBOK® Guide* – **Third Edition**)

Control Account Plan (CAP) [Tool]

A plan for all the work and effort to be performed in a control account. Each CAP has a definitive statement of work, schedule, and time-phased budget. Previously called a Cost Account Plan. (*PMBOK® Guide* – **Third Edition**)

Control Chart [Tool]

A graphic display of process data over time and against established control limits, and that has a centerline that assists in detecting a trend of plotted values toward either control limit. (*PMBOK® Guide* – **Third Edition**)

Combined Standards Glossary
©2007 Project Management Institute, Four Campus Boulevard, Newtown Square, PA 19073-3299 USA

Control Limits

The area composed of three standard deviations on either side of the centerline, or mean, of a normal distribution of data plotted on a control chart that reflects the expected variation in the data. (*PMBOK® Guide* – **Third Edition**)

> SEE ALSO   Specification Limits
> (*PMBOK® Guide* – **Third Edition**)

Controlling

> SEE   Control (*PMBOK® Guide* – **Third Edition**)

Corporate Governance

The process by which an organization directs and controls its operational and strategic activities, and by which the organization responds to the legitimate rights, expectations, and desires of its stakeholders. (*Program Management*)

Corrective Action

Documented direction for executing the project work to bring expected future performance of the project work in line with the project management plan. (*PMBOK® Guide* – **Third Edition**)

Cost

The monetary value or price of a project activity or component that includes the monetary worth of the resources required to perform and complete the activity or component, or to produce the component. A specific cost can be composed of a combination of cost components including direct labor hours, other direct costs, indirect labor hours, other indirect costs, and purchased price. (However, in the earned value management methodology, in some instances, the term cost can represent only labor hours without conversion to monetary worth.) (*PMBOK® Guide* – **Third Edition**)

> SEE ALSO   Actual Cost (AC)
> (*PMBOK® Guide* – **Third Edition**)
> Estimate (*PMBOK® Guide* – **Third Edition**)

Cost Baseline

> SEE   Baseline (*PMBOK® Guide* – **Third Edition**)

Cost Budgeting [Process]

The process of aggregating the estimated costs of individual activities or work packages to establish a cost baseline. (*PMBOK® Guide* – **Third Edition**)

Combined Standards Glossary
©2007 Project Management Institute, Four Campus Boulevard, Newtown Square, PA 19073-3299 USA

Cost Control [Process]

The process of influencing the factors that create variances, and controlling changes to the project budget. (*PMBOK® Guide* – **Third Edition**)

Cost Estimating [Process]

The process of developing an approximation of the cost of the resources needed to complete project activities. (*PMBOK® Guide* – **Third Edition**)

Cost Management Plan [Output/Input]

The document that sets out the format and establishes the activities and criteria for planning, structuring, and controlling the project costs. A cost management plan can be formal or informal, highly detailed or broadly framed, based on the requirements of the project stakeholders. The cost management plan is contained in, or is a subsidiary plan, of the project management plan. (*PMBOK® Guide* – **Third Edition**)

Cost of Quality (COQ) [Technique]

Determining the costs incurred to ensure quality. Prevention and appraisal costs (cost of conformance) include costs for quality planning, quality control (QC), and quality assurance to ensure compliance to requirements (i.e., training, QC systems, etc.). Failure costs (cost of non-conformance) include costs to rework products, components, or processes that are non-compliant, costs of warranty work and waste, and loss of reputation. (*PMBOK® Guide* – **Third Edition**)

Cost Performance Index (CPI)

A measure of cost efficiency on a project. It is the ratio of earned value (EV) to actual costs (AC). CPI = EV divided by AC. A value equal to or greater than one indicates a favorable condition and a value less than one indicates an unfavorable condition. (*PMBOK® Guide* – **Third Edition**) (*PS-EVM*)

Cost-Plus-Fee (CPF)

A type of cost reimbursable contract where the buyer reimburses the seller for seller's allowable costs for performing the contract work and seller also receives a fee calculated as an agreed upon percentage of the costs. The fee varies with the actual cost. (*PMBOK® Guide* – **Third Edition**)

Cost-Plus-Fixed Fee (CPFF) Contract

A type of cost-reimbursable contract where the buyer reimburses the seller for the seller's allowable costs (allowable costs are defined by the contract) plus a fixed amount of profit (fee). (*PMBOK® Guide* – **Third Edition**)

Cost-Plus-Incentive Fee (CPIF) Contract

A type of cost-reimbursable contract where the buyer reimburses the seller for the seller's allowable costs (allowable costs are defined by the contract), and the seller earns its profit if it meets defined performance criteria. (*PMBOK® Guide* – **Third Edition**)

Cost-Plus-Percentage of Cost (CPPC)

SEE   Cost-Plus-Fee (CPF) (*PMBOK® Guide* – **Third Edition**)

Cost-Reimbursable Contract

A type of contract involving payment (reimbursement) by the buyer to the seller for the seller's actual costs, plus a fee typically representing seller's profit. Costs are usually classified as direct costs or indirect costs. Direct costs are costs incurred for the exclusive benefit of the project, such as salaries of full-time project staff. Indirect costs, also called overhead and general and administrative cost, are costs allocated to the project by the performing organization as a cost of doing business, such as salaries of management indirectly involved in the project, and cost of electric utilities for the office. Indirect costs are usually calculated as a percentage of direct costs. Cost-reimbursable contracts often include incentive clauses where, if the seller meets or exceeds selected project objectives, such as schedule targets or total cost, then the seller receives from the buyer an incentive or bonus payment. (*PMBOK® Guide* – **Third Edition**)

Cost Variance (CV)

A measure of cost performance on a project. It is the algebraic difference between earned value (EV) and actual cost (AC). CV = EV minus AC. A positive value indicates a favorable condition and a negative value indicates an unfavorable condition. (*PMBOK® Guide* – **Third Edition**) (*PS-EVM*)

Crashing [Technique]

A specific type of project schedule compression technique performed by taking action to decrease the total project schedule duration after analyzing a number of alternatives to determine how to get the maximum schedule duration compression for the least additional cost. Typical approaches for crashing a schedule include reducing schedule activity durations and increasing the assignment of resources on schedule activities. (*PMBOK® Guide* – **Third Edition**)

SEE ALSO   Fast Tracking
(*PMBOK® Guide* – **Third Edition**)
Schedule Compression
(*PMBOK® Guide* – **Third Edition**)

Create WBS (Work Breakdown Structure) [Process]

The process of subdividing the major project deliverables and project work into smaller, more manageable components. (*PMBOK® Guide* – **Third Edition**)

Criteria

Standards, rules, or tests on which a judgment or decision can be based, or by which a product, service, result, or process can be evaluated. (*PMBOK® Guide* – **Third Edition**)

Critical Activity

Any schedule activity on a critical path in a project schedule. Most commonly determined by using the critical path method. Although some activities are "critical," in the dictionary sense, without being on the critical path, this meaning is seldom used in the project context. (*PMBOK® Guide* – **Third Edition**)

Critical Chain Method [Technique]

A schedule network analysis technique that modifies the project schedule to account for limited resources. The critical chain method mixes deterministic and probabilistic approaches to schedule network analysis. (*PMBOK® Guide* – **Third Edition**)

Critical Path [Output/Input]

Generally, but not always, the sequence of schedule activities that determines the duration of the project. Generally, it is the longest path through the project. However, a critical path can end, as an example, on a schedule milestone that is in the middle of the project schedule and that has a finish-no-later-than imposed date schedule constraint. (*PMBOK® Guide* – **Third Edition**)

SEE ALSO   Critical Path Method (CPM)
(*PMBOK® Guide* – **Third Edition**)

Critical Path Method (CPM) [Technique]

A schedule network analysis technique used to determine the amount of scheduling flexibility (the amount of float) on various logical network paths in the project schedule network, and to determine the minimum total project duration. Early start and finish dates are calculated by means of a forward pass, using a specified start date. Late start and finish dates are calculated by means of a backward pass, starting from a specified completion date, which sometimes is the project early finish date determined during the forward pass calculation. (*PMBOK® Guide* – **Third Edition**)

Combined Standards Glossary
©2007 Project Management Institute, Four Campus Boulevard, Newtown Square, PA 19073-3299 USA

Currency Hedging

A way of limiting exposure to future changes in the exchange rate of currencies. (*Const Ext*)

Current Finish Date

The current estimate of the point in time when a schedule activity will be completed, where the estimate reflects any reported work progress. (*PMBOK® Guide* – **Third Edition**)

> SEE ALSO Baseline Finish Date
> (*PMBOK® Guide* – **Third Edition**)
> Scheduled Finish Date (SF)
> (*PMBOK® Guide* – **Third Edition**)

Current Start Date

The current estimate of the point in time when a schedule activity will begin, where the estimate reflects any reported work progress. (*PMBOK® Guide* – **Third Edition**)

> SEE ALSO Baseline Start Date
> (*PMBOK® Guide* – **Third Edition**)
> Scheduled Start Date (SS)
> (*PMBOK® Guide* – **Third Edition**)

Customer

1) The person or organization that will use the project's product or service or result. (*PMBOK® Guide* – **Third Edition**)(*PS-WBS*)
2) The person or organization that will use the program's benefits, products or services or result. (*Program Management*)

> SEE ALSO User (*PMBOK® Guide* – **Third Edition**)(*PS-WBS*)

Data Date (DD)

The date up to or through which the project's reporting system has provided actual status and accomplishments. In some reporting systems, the status information for the data date is included in the past and in some systems the status information is in the future. Also called as-of date and time-now date. (*PMBOK® Guide* – **Third Edition**)

Date

A term representing the day, month, and year of a calendar, and, in some instances, the time of day. (*PMBOK® Guide* – **Third Edition**)

Decision Tree Analysis [Technique]

The decision tree is a diagram that describes a decision under consideration and the implications of choosing one or another of the available alternatives. It is used when some future scenarios or outcomes of actions are uncertain. It incorporates probabilities and the costs or

Combined Standards Glossary
©2007 Project Management Institute, Four Campus Boulevard, Newtown Square, PA 19073-3299 USA

rewards of each logical path of events and future decisions, and uses expected monetary value analysis to help the organization identify the relative values of alternate actions. (*PMBOK® Guide* – **Third Edition**)

> SEE ALSO   Expected Monetary Value (EMV) Analysis (*PMBOK® Guide* – **Third Edition**)

Decompose

> SEE   Decomposition (*PMBOK® Guide* – **Third Edition**)

Decomposition [Technique]

1) A planning technique that subdivides the project scope and project deliverables into smaller, more manageable components, until the project work associated with accomplishing the project scope and providing the deliverables is defined in sufficient detail to support executing, monitoring, and controlling the work. (*PMBOK® Guide* – **Third Edition**)(*PS-WBS*)

2) Decomposition involves subdividing the major project deliverables into smaller, more manageable components until the deliverables are defined in sufficient detail to support future project activities (planning, executing, controlling, and closing). (*PS-WBS*)

Defect

An imperfection or deficiency in a project component where that component does not meet its requirements or specifications and needs to be either repaired or replaced. (*PMBOK® Guide* – **Third Edition**)

Defect Repair

Formally documented identification of a defect in a project component with a recommendation to either repair the defect or completely replace the component. (*PMBOK® Guide* – **Third Edition**)

Defined Contribution

Split funding by program where some fund source(s) contribute a fixed amount, with one source funding the balance. (*Gov't Ext*)

> SEE ALSO   Fund Source (*Gov't Ext*)

Defined Elements of Work

Split funding by program where each program bears the cost of its portion(s) of the project on a percentage basis. (*Gov't Ext*)

> SEE ALSO   Fund Source (*Gov't Ext*)

Deliverable [Output/Input]

Any unique and verifiable product, result, or capability to perform a service that must be produced to complete a process, phase, or project. Often used more narrowly in reference to an external deliverable, which

Combined Standards Glossary
©2007 Project Management Institute, Four Campus Boulevard, Newtown Square, PA 19073-3299 USA

is a deliverable that is subject to approval by the project sponsor or customer. (*PMBOK® Guide* – **Third Edition**)(*PS-WBS*)

SEE ALSO   Product (*PMBOK® Guide* – **Third Edition**)
Result (*PMBOK® Guide* – **Third Edition**)
Service (*PMBOK® Guide* – **Third Edition**)

Delphi Technique [Technique]

An information gathering technique used as a way to reach a consensus of experts on a subject. Experts on the subject participate in this technique anonymously. A facilitator uses a questionnaire to solicit ideas about the important project points related to the subject. The responses are summarized and are then re-circulated to the experts for further comment. Consensus may be reached in a few rounds of this process. The Delphi technique helps reduce bias in the data and keeps any one person from having undue influence on the outcome. (*PMBOK® Guide* – **Third Edition**)

Delivery Systems

Various methods of performing design/construction projects such as design-bid-build and design-build. (*Const Ext*)

Dependencies

Dependencies are relationships in which a desired state is contingent upon the achievement of one or more prerequisites.

One type of Dependency in OPM3 is represented by the series of Capabilities that aggregate to a Best Practice. In general, each Capability builds upon preceding Capabilities.

Another type of Dependency occurs when the existence of one Best Practice depends, in part, on the existence of some other Best Practice. In this case, at least one of the Capabilities within the first Best Practice depends on the existence of one of the Capabilities within the other Best Practice. (*OPM3*)

SEE ALSO   Interdependencies (*OPM3*)

Dependency

SEE   Logical Relationship (*PMBOK® Guide* – **Third Edition**)

Dependency Relationship

SEE   Dependencies (*OPM3*)

Design-Bid-Build

Design is completed by a professional architect or engineer; a construction contract is awarded after competitive bids. (*Const Ext*)

Design-Build

A single entity performs both design and construction of the project. (*Const Ext*)

Design-Build-Operate-Maintain (DBOM)

Similar to DBOO except that the design builder has no ownership of the project. (*Const Ext*)

Design Review [Technique]

A management technique used for evaluating a proposed design to ensure that the design of the system or product meets the customer requirements, or to assure that the design will perform successfully, can be produced, and can be maintained. (*PMBOK® Guide* – **Third Edition**)

Determining Factors

Key descriptors of the portfolio such as component definition, category definition, key criteria definition, and resources capacity to support the portfolio management process. The determining factors are agreed upon by the executive group and are based on the organization strategic plan. (*Portfolio Management*)

Develop Project Charter [Process]

The process of developing the project charter that formally authorizes a project. (*PMBOK® Guide* – **Third Edition**)

Develop Project Management Plan [Process]

The process of documenting the actions necessary to define, prepare, integrate, and coordinate all subsidiary plans into a project management plan. (*PMBOK® Guide* – **Third Edition**)

Develop Project Scope Statement (Preliminary) [Process]

The process of developing the preliminary project scope statement that provides a high level scope narrative. (*PMBOK® Guide* – **Third Edition**)

Develop Project Team [Process]

The process of improving the competencies and interaction of team members to enhance project performance. (*PMBOK® Guide* – **Third Edition**)

Devolution

Delegation of work or power by a national government to a regional or local government; or by a regional government to a local government. (*Gov't Ext*)

Devolve

SEE   Devolution (*Gov't Ext*)

Combined Standards Glossary
©2007 Project Management Institute, Four Campus Boulevard, Newtown Square, PA 19073-3299 USA

Direct and Manage Project Execution [Process]

The process of executing the work defined in the project management plan to achieve the project's requirements defined in the project scope statement. (*PMBOK® Guide* – **Third Edition**)

Discipline

A field of work requiring specific knowledge and that has a set of rules governing work conduct (e.g., mechanical engineering, computer programming, cost estimating, etc.). (*PMBOK® Guide* – **Third Edition**)

Discrete Effort

1) *Work effort* that is separate, distinct, and related to the completion of specific *work breakdown structure* components and *deliverables*, and that can be directly planned and measured. Contrast with *apportioned effort*. (*PMBOK® Guide* – **Third Edition**)

2) Work effort that is separate, distinct, and related to the completion of specific end products or services, and that can be directly planned and measured. (Note: The *PMBOK® Guide* – Third Edition definition for this term is broader and more inclusive in that it applies beyond the scope of the *Practice Standard for Earned Value Management*.) (*PS-EVM*)

Dispute Review Board

A board formed at the start of or early in the project to review and adjudicate any disputes that may arise. (***Const Ext***)

Document

A medium and the information recorded thereon, that generally has permanence and can be read by a person or a machine. Examples include project management plans, specifications, procedures, studies, and manuals. (*PMBOK® Guide* – **Third Edition**)

Documented Procedure

A formalized written description of how to carry out an activity, process, technique, or methodology. (*PMBOK® Guide* – **Third Edition**)

Domain

A Domain refers to the three distinct disciplines of Portfolio Management, Program Management, and Project Management (also referred to as PPP). (***OPM3***)

SEE ALSO   Project (***OPM3***)
Program (***OPM3***)
Portfolio (***OPM3***)
PPP (***OPM3***)

Combined Standards Glossary
©2007 Project Management Institute, Four Campus Boulevard, Newtown Square, PA 19073-3299 USA

Dummy Activity

A schedule activity of zero duration used to show a logical relationship in the arrow diagramming method. Dummy activities are used when logical relationships cannot be completely or correctly described with schedule activity arrows. Dummy activities are generally shown graphically as a dashed line headed by an arrow. (*PMBOK® Guide* – **Third Edition**)

Duration (DU or DUR)

The total number of work periods (not including holidays or other nonworking periods) required to complete a schedule activity or work breakdown structure component. Usually expressed as workdays or workweeks. Sometimes incorrectly equated with elapsed time. Contrast with *effort.* (*PMBOK® Guide* – **Third Edition**)

> SEE ALSO   Actual Duration
> (*PMBOK® Guide* – **Third Edition**)
> Original Duration (OD)
> (*PMBOK® Guide* – **Third Edition**)
> Remaining Duration (RD)
> (*PMBOK® Guide* – **Third Edition**)

Early Finish Date (EF)

In the critical path method, the earliest possible point in time on which the uncompleted portions of a schedule activity (or the project) can finish, based on the schedule network logic, the data date, and any schedule constraints. Early finish dates can change as the project progresses and as changes are made to the project management plan. (*PMBOK® Guide* – **Third Edition**)

Early Start Date (ES)

In the critical path method, the earliest possible point in time on which the uncompleted portions of a schedule activity (or the project) can start, based on the schedule network logic, the data date, and any schedule constraints. Early start dates can change as the project progresses and as changes are made to the project management plan. (*PMBOK® Guide* – **Third Edition**)

Earned Value (EV)

1) The value of *work* performed expressed in terms of the approved *budget* assigned to that work for a *schedule activity* or *work breakdown structure component.* Also referred to as the *budgeted cost of work performed* (BCWP). (*PMBOK® Guide* – **Third Edition**)

2) The value of work performed expressed in terms of the budget assigned to that work. Also referred to as the Budgeted Cost of Work Performed (BCWP). (Note: The *PMBOK® Guide* – Third Edition

definition for this term is broader and more inclusive in that it applies beyond the scope of the *Practice Standard for Earned Value Management*.) (***PS-EVM***)

Earned Value Management (EVM)

A management methodology for integrating scope, schedule, and resources, and for objectively measuring project performance and progress. Performance is measured by determining the budgeted cost of work performed (i.e., earned value) and comparing it to the actual cost of work performed (i.e., actual cost). Progress is measured by comparing the earned value to the planned value. (***PMBOK® Guide – Third Edition***)

Earned Value Technique (EVT) [Technique]

1) A specific technique for measuring the performance of work and used to establish the *performance measurement baseline* (PMB). Also referred to as the earning rules and crediting method. (***PMBOK® Guide – Third Edition***)
2) A technique or method for measuring the performance of work, and used to establish the performance measurement baseline (PMB). (Note: The *PMBOK® Guide* – Third Edition definition for this term is broader and more inclusive in that it applies beyond the scope of the *Practice Standard for Earned Value Management*.) (***PS-EVM***)

Effective Performance

An intended or expected accomplishment. (***PMCDF***)

Effort

The number of labor units required to complete a schedule activity or work breakdown structure component. Usually expressed as staff hours, staff days, or staff weeks. Contrast with *duration*. (***PMBOK® Guide – Third Edition***)

Eichleay Formula

A U.S. government method of calculating overhead due on certain changes. (***Const Ext***)

Elements of Competence

The basic building blocks of the Unit of Competence. They describe, in output terms, actions or outcomes, which are demonstrable and assessable. (***PMCDF***)

Eminent Domain

A process that allows the government to take possession of private property when this is deemed to be in the best interests of the public. (***Gov't Ext***)

Encumbrance

SEE Obligation (*Gov't Ext*)

Enterprise

A company, business, firm, partnership, corporation, or governmental agency. (*PMBOK® Guide* – **Third Edition**)

Enterprise Environmental Factors [Output/Input]

Any or all external environmental factors and internal organizational environmental factors that surround or influence the project's success. These factors are from any or all of the enterprises involved in the project, and include organizational culture and structure, infrastructure, existing resources, commercial databases, market conditions, and project management software. (*PMBOK® Guide* – **Third Edition**)

Environmental Review

A process in which potential impacts to natural, cultural, historical, and community resources are identified and examined, and strategies are developed to mitigate any significant impacts. Environmental review typically culminates in the production of one or more environmental documents (e.g., EIR. (*Gov't Ext*)

Estimate [Output/Input]

A quantitative assessment of the likely amount or outcome. Usually applied to project costs, resources, effort, and durations and is usually preceded by a modifier (i.e., preliminary, conceptual, feasibility, order-of-magnitude, definitive). It should always include some indication of accuracy (e.g., ±x percent). (*PMBOK® Guide* – **Third Edition**)

Estimate at Completion (EAC) [Output/Input]

1) The expected total cost of a schedule activity, a work breakdown structure component, or the project when the defined scope of work will be completed. EAC is equal to the actual cost (AC) plus the estimate to complete (ETC) for all of the remaining work. EAC = AC plus ETC. The EAC may be calculated based on performance to date or estimated by the project team based on other factors, in which case it is often referred to as the latest revised estimate. (*PMBOK® Guide* – **Third Edition**)

2) The expected total cost of completing project work. EAC is equal to the actual cost (AC) plus the estimate to complete (ETC) for all of the remaining work. The EAC may be calculated based on performance to date or estimated by the project team based on other factors. (Note: The *PMBOK® Guide* – Third Edition definition for this term is broader and more inclusive in that it applies beyond

Combined Standards Glossary
©2007 Project Management Institute, Four Campus Boulevard, Newtown Square, PA 19073-3299 USA

the scope of the *Practice Standard for Earned Value Management.*)
(PS-EVM)

SEE ALSO Earned Value Technique (EVT)
(PMBOK® Guide – Third Edition)
Estimate to Complete (ETC)
(PMBOK® Guide – Third Edition)

Estimate to Complete (ETC) [Output/Input]

1) The expected cost needed to complete all the remaining work for a schedule activity, work breakdown structure component, or the project. **(PMBOK® Guide – Third Edition)**
2) The estimated cost of completing the remaining work. (Note: The *PMBOK® Guide* – Third Edition definition for this term is broader and more inclusive in that it applies beyond the scope of the *Practice Standard for Earned Value Management.*) **(PS-EVM)**

SEE ALSO Earned Value Technique (EVT)
(PMBOK® Guide – Third Edition)
Estimate at Completion (EAC)
(PMBOK® Guide – Third Edition)

Evaluation

The process of scoring specific potential components using key indicators and their related weighted criteria for comparison purpose for further decision-making. **(Portfolio Management)**

Event

Something that happens, an occurrence, an outcome. **(PMBOK® Guide – Third Edition)**

Exception Report

Document that includes only major variations from the plan (rather than all variations). **(PMBOK® Guide – Third Edition)**

Execute

Directing, managing, performing, and accomplishing the project work, providing the deliverables, and providing work performance information. **(PMBOK® Guide – Third Edition)**

Executing

SEE Execute **(PMBOK® Guide – Third Edition)**

Executing Processes [Process Group]

1) Those processes performed to complete the work defined in the project management plan to accomplish the project's objectives defined in the project scope statement. **(PMBOK® Guide – Third Edition)**

2) Those processes performed to complete the work defined in the program management plan to accomplish the program's objectives defined in its scope statement. (***Program Management***)

Execution

SEE   Execute (***PMBOK® Guide* – Third Edition**)

Exit Interviews

Interviews of construction (and project) staff as they leave the project. (***Const Ext***)

Expected Monetary Value (EMV) Analysis

A statistical technique that calculates the average outcome when the future includes scenarios that may or may not happen. A common use of this technique is within decision tree analysis. Modeling and simulation are recommended for cost and schedule risk analysis because it is more powerful and less subject to misapplication than expected monetary value analysis. (***PMBOK® Guide* – Third Edition**)

Expert Judgment [Technique]

Judgment provided based upon expertise in an application area, knowledge area, discipline, industry, etc. as appropriate for the activity being performed. Such expertise may be provided by any group or person with specialized education, knowledge, skill, experience, or training, and is available from many sources, including: other units within the performing organization; consultants; stakeholders, including customers; professional and technical associations; and industry groups. (***PMBOK® Guide* – Third Edition**)

Failure Mode and Effect Analysis (FMEA) [Technique]

An analytical procedure in which each potential failure mode in every component of a product is analyzed to determine its effect on the reliability of that component and, by itself or in combination with other possible failure modes, on the reliability of the product or system and on the required function of the component; or the examination of a product (at the system and/or lower levels) for all ways that a failure may occur. For each potential failure, an estimate is made of its effect on the total system and of its impact. In addition, a review is undertaken of the action planned to minimize the probability of failure and to minimize its effects. (***PMBOK® Guide* – Third Edition**)

Fast Tracking [Technique]

A specific project schedule compression technique that changes network logic to overlap phases that would normally be done in sequence, such as the design phase and construction phase, or to perform schedule activities in parallel. (***PMBOK® Guide* – Third Edition**)

Combined Standards Glossary
©2007 Project Management Institute, Four Campus Boulevard, Newtown Square, PA 19073-3299 USA

Feasibility Study

An early engineering and financial analysis of a proposed project to determine its viability. (***Const Ext***)

Filter

Criteria used to evaluate and select a potential component or decide whether a component meets the "go/no go" conditions. (***Portfolio Management***)

Finish Date

A point in time associated with a schedule activity's completion. Usually qualified by one of the following: actual, planned, estimated, scheduled, early, late, baseline, target, or current. (*PMBOK® Guide* – **Third Edition**)

Finish-to-Finish (FF)

The logical relationship where completion of work of the successor activity cannot finish until the completion of work of the predecessor activity. (*PMBOK® Guide* – **Third Edition**)

SEE ALSO   Logical Relationship
(*PMBOK® Guide* – **Third Edition**)

Finish-to-Start (FS)

The logical relationship where initiation of work of the successor activity depends upon the completion of work of the predecessor activity. (*PMBOK® Guide* – **Third Edition**)

SEE ALSO   Logical Relationship
(*PMBOK® Guide* – **Third Edition**)

Firm-Fixed-Price (FFP) Contract

A type of fixed price contract where the buyer pays the seller a set amount (as defined by the contract), regardless of the seller's costs. (*PMBOK® Guide* – **Third Edition**)

Fixed-Price-Incentive-Fee (FPIF) Contract

A type of contract where the buyer pays the seller a set amount (as defined by the contract), and the seller can earn an additional amount if the seller meets defined performance criteria. (*PMBOK® Guide* – **Third Edition**)

Fixed-Price or Lump-Sum Contract

A type of contract involving a fixed total price for a well-defined product. Fixed-price contracts may also include incentives for meeting or exceeding selected project objectives, such as schedule targets. The simplest form of a fixed price contract is a purchase order. (*PMBOK®* *Guide* – **Third Edition**)

Float

Also called slack. (*PMBOK® Guide* – **Third Edition**)

SEE ALSO   Free Float (FF)
              (*PMBOK® Guide* – **Third Edition**)
              Total Float (TF)
              (*PMBOK® Guide* – **Third Edition**)

Flowcharting [Technique]

The depiction in a diagram format of the inputs, process actions, and outputs of one or more processes within a system. (*PMBOK® Guide* – **Third Edition**)

Force Majeure

An event not reasonably anticipated and acts of God such as weather, strikes or other uncontrollable events. (*Const Ext*)

Forecasts

Estimates or predictions of conditions and events in the project's future based on information and knowledge available at the time of the forecast. Forecasts are updated and reissued based on work performance information provided as the project is executed. The information is based on the project's past performance and expected future performance, and includes information that could impact the project in the future, such as estimate at completion and estimate to complete. (*PMBOK® Guide* – **Third Edition**)

Forward Pass

The calculation of the early start and early finish dates for the uncompleted portions of all network activities. (*PMBOK® Guide* – **Third Edition**)

SEE ALSO   Backward Pass
              (*PMBOK® Guide* – **Third Edition**)
              Schedule Network Analysis
              (*PMBOK® Guide* – **Third Edition**)

Free Float (FF)

The amount of time that a schedule activity can be delayed without delaying the early start of any immediately following schedule activities. (*PMBOK® Guide* – **Third Edition**)

SEE ALSO   Total Float (TF)
              (*PMBOK® Guide* – **Third Edition**)

Fringe Benefits

Costs of labor beyond wages, such as vacation, holidays, insurance and taxes. (*Const Ext*)

Full and Open Competition

A process in which all responsible sources are allowed to compete for a contract. (*Gov't Ext*)

Full and Open Competition After Exclusion of Sources

A process in which agencies are allowed to exclude one or more sources from competing for a contract. A set-aside for a small business or small disadvantaged firms is an example of this method. (*Gov't Ext*)

Functional Manager

Someone with management authority over an organizational unit within a functional organization. The manager of any group that actually makes a product or performs a service. Sometimes called a line manager. (*PMBOK® Guide* – **Third Edition**)

Functional Organization

A hierarchical organization where each employee has one clear superior, staff are grouped by areas of specialization, and managed by a person with expertise in that area. (*PMBOK® Guide* – **Third Edition**)

Funds

A supply of money or pecuniary resources immediately available. (*PMBOK® Guide* – **Third Edition**)

Fund Source

A source of funding for a government project. A project may have more than one fund source. Fund sources may include national, regional, and local governments, as well as other sources (e.g., banks and financial institutions). (*Gov't Ext*)

Gantt Chart

SEE   Bar Chart (*PMBOK® Guide* – **Third Edition**)

General Contractor

A contractor who does not specialize in one kind of work. Often the major contractor who employs specialty subcontractors. (*Const Ext*)

Goods

Commodities, wares, merchandise. (*PMBOK® Guide* – **Third Edition**)

Government Body

An assembly of people at the national, regional or local level, which deliberates and establishes applicable laws or regulations and administers government projects. In some jurisdictions, laws or regulations may also be known as "statutes" and "ordinances." (***Gov't Ext***)

Government Transfer Payment
SEE   Obligation (***Gov't Ext***)

Grade
A category or rank used to distinguish items that have the same functional use (e.g., "hammer"), but do not share the same requirements for quality (e.g., different hammers may need to withstand different amounts of force). (***PMBOK® Guide** – **Third Edition***)

Ground Rules [Tool]
A list of acceptable and unacceptable behaviors adopted by a project team to improve working relationships, effectiveness, and communication. (***PMBOK® Guide** – **Third Edition***)

Hammock Activity
SEE   Summary Activity (***PMBOK® Guide** – **Third Edition***)

Hazard Analysis
A review of all the safety hazards that may be encountered in a project. Used to form a safety plan. (***Const Ext***)

Historical Information
Documents and data on prior projects including project files, records, correspondence, closed contracts, and closed projects. (***PMBOK® Guide** – **Third Edition***)

Human Resource Planning [Process]
The process of identifying and documenting project roles, responsibilities and reporting relationships, as well as creating the staffing management plan. (***PMBOK® Guide** – **Third Edition***)

Hybrid Staff
A mixture of civil service and contracted staff. (***Gov't Ext***)

Identificaiton
The process of documenting and assembling, for further decision-making, the inventory of ongoing and proposed new components as potential components for categorization. (***Portfolio Management***)

Imposed Date
A fixed date imposed on a schedule activity or schedule milestone, usually in the form of a "start no earlier than" and "finish no later than" date. (***PMBOK® Guide** – **Third Edition***)

Improvement Planning Directory

The Improvement Planning Directory contains a checklist of Capabilities, in priority order, that are necessary to establish the achievement of a Best Practice. For each Capability, there is a column for the user to check off the existence of each of the Outcomes associated with that Capability.

For each Best Practice, the checklist includes the Capability ID Numbers and Names defined within the Best Practice (Intradependencies), as well as any ID Numbers and Names of Capabilities that are prerequisites to achieving the Best Practice, but have been defined within, and are primarily associated with, other Best Practices (Interdependencies). The Interdependencies are identified by having both a different Capability ID Number that starts with the Best Practice Number within which it can be found, and a different font color).

These Capabilities/Outcomes are in the recommended sequence by which the various Capabilities aggregate to the Best Practice. The Improvement Planning Directory thus serves as a suggested path by which an organization can approach improvements in maturity by achieving Outcomes associated with Capabilities, in priority order, to attain Best Practices. The Improvement Planning Directory appears in an appendix to the *OPM3*. (*OPM3*)

Indefinite Delivery Indefinite Quantity (IDIQ) Contracts

Contracts that states the type of service to be delivered, the length of time in which the service can be requested (generally five years or less), and the minimum and maximum contract amount, but give no project-specific information. Additionally, the contract typically includes a "price book" and each potential seller submits a markup or markdown in the form of a coefficient (e.g., 1.1. or 0.9). (*Gov't Ext*)

Influence Diagram [Tool]

Graphical representation of situations showing causal influences, time ordering of events, and other relationships among variables and outcomes. (*PMBOK® Guide* – **Third Edition**)

Influencer

Persons or groups that are not directly related to the acquisition or use of the project's product, but, due to their position in the customer organization, can influence, positively or negatively, the course of the project. (*PMBOK® Guide* – **Third Edition**)

Information Distribution [Process]

The process of making needed information available to project stakeholders in a timely manner. (*PMBOK® Guide* – **Third Edition**)

Initiating Processes [Process Group]

1) Those processes performed to authorize and define the scope of a new phase or project or that can result in the continuation of halted project work. A large number of the initiating processes are typically done outside the project's scope of control by the organization, program, or portfolio processes and those processes provide input to the project's initiating processes group. (*PMBOK® Guide* – **Third Edition**)

2) Those processes performed to authorize and define the scope of a new phase or program, or that can result in the continuation of halted program work. (*Program Management*)

Initiator

A person or organization that has both the ability and authority to start a project. (*PMBOK® Guide* – **Third Edition**)

Input [Process Input]

1) Any item, whether internal or external to the project that is required by a process before that process proceeds. May be an output from a predecessor process. (*PMBOK® Guide* – **Third Edition**)

2) A document or documentable item that will be acted upon by a process. (*OPM3*)

3) Any item, whether internal or external to the program, that is required by a process before that process proceeds. May be an output from a predecessor process. (*Program Management*)

Inspection [Technique]

Examining or measuring to verify whether an activity, component, product, result or service conforms to specified requirements. (*PMBOK® Guide* – **Third Edition**)

Inventory

A set of components, comprising all active components as well as proposals for new components, properly documented using key descriptors, use as a basis for portfolio management decision-making. (*Portfolio Management*)

Integral

Essential to completeness; requisite; constituent with; formed as a unit with another component. (*PMBOK® Guide* – **Third Edition**)

Integrated

Interrelated, interconnected, interlocked, or meshed components blended and unified into a functioning or unified whole. (*PMBOK® Guide* – **Third Edition**)

Combined Standards Glossary
©2007 Project Management Institute, Four Campus Boulevard, Newtown Square, PA 19073-3299 USA

Integrated Change Control [Process]

The process of reviewing all change requests, approving changes and controlling changes to deliverables and organizational process assets. (*PMBOK® Guide* – **Third Edition**)

Intent

The motive or trait force that is the basis that may result in, or cause action toward, an outcome. (*PMCDF*)

Interdependencies

Interdependencies reflect the general relationship between Capabilities and Best Practices. They suggest the sequence in which the organization should develop the underlying Capabilities that support associated Best Practices. (*OPM3*)

Interrelationships

Interrelationships are logical relationships that define the normal flow of information between Project Management Processes. (*OPM3*)

Invitation for Bid (IFB)

Generally, this term is equivalent to request for proposal. However, in some application areas, it may have a narrower or more specific meaning. (*PMBOK® Guide* – **Third Edition**)

Issue

A point or matter in question or in dispute, or a point or matter that is not settled and is under discussion or over which there are opposing views or disagreements. (*PMBOK® Guide* – **Third Edition**)

Job Description

A description of the responsibilities and authorities of an employee. (*Const Ext*)

Job Order Contract (JOC)

SEE   IDIQ Contracts (*Gov't Ext*)

Joint Venture

A partnership of two or more engineering, construction, manufacturing trading, or investing companies, often of limited duration. (*Const Ext*)

Key Criteria

Predetermined measures, values or conditions used in a scoring model to measure alignment with strategic goals. (*Portfolio Management*)

Key Descriptors

A set of characteristics used to categorize and document a component for further decision-making. It might include among others, specifics about

Combined Standards Glossary
©2007 Project Management Institute, Four Campus Boulevard, Newtown Square, PA 19073-3299 USA

scope, schedule, budget, actual performance (using key performance indicators), class, category, evaluation scores, priority, and approval status. (***Portfolio Management***)

Key Indicators

A set of parameters that permits visibility into how a component measures up to a given criterion. (***Portfolio Management***)

Key Performance Indicator (KPI)

1) A Key Performance Indicator (KPI) is a criterion by which an organization can determine, quantitatively or qualitatively, whether the Outcome associated with a Capability exists or the degree to which it exists. A Key Performance Indicator can be a direct measurement or an expert assessment.

When a Key Performance Indicator is quantitative, involving direct measurement, a form of metric is required. A metric is a measurement of something. Something tangible, such as an error count, can be measured directly and objectively. Something intangible, such as customer satisfaction, must first be made tangible—for example, through a survey resulting in ratings on a scale—before it can be measured. A metric can be binary (something exists or does not exist), it can be more complex (such as a scaled rating), or it can be monetary (such as financial return). (***OPM3***)

2) A set of parameters that permits visibility into how a component measures up to a given criterion. (***Portfolio Management***)

Knowledge

1) Knowing something with the familiarity gained through experience, education, observation, or investigation, it is understanding a process, practice, or technique, or how to use a tool. (***PMBOK® Guide* – Third Edition**)
2) A body of information (conceptual, factual, procedural) that can be directly applied to the performance of tasks. (***PMCDF***)

Knowledge Area Process

An identifiable project management process within a knowledge area. (***PMBOK® Guide* – Third Edition**)

Knowledge Area, Project Management

SEE   Project Management Knowledge Area
(***PMBOK® Guide* – Third Edition**)

Lag [Technique]

A modification of a logical relationship that directs a delay in the successor activity. For example, in a finish-to-start dependency with a

Combined Standards Glossary
©2007 Project Management Institute, Four Campus Boulevard, Newtown Square, PA 19073-3299 USA

ten-day lag, the successor activity cannot start until ten days after the predecessor activity has finished. (***PMBOK® Guide* – Third Edition**)

SEE ALSO   Lead (***PMBOK® Guide* – Third Edition**)

Late Finish Date (LF)

In the critical path method, the latest possible point in time that a schedule activity may be completed based upon the schedule network logic, the project completion date, and any constraints assigned to the schedule activities without violating a schedule constraint or delaying the project completion date. The late finish dates are determined during the backward pass calculation of the project schedule network. (***PMBOK® Guide* – Third Edition**)

Late Start Date (LS)

In the critical path method, the latest possible point in time that a schedule activity may begin based upon the schedule network logic, the project completion date, and any constraints assigned to the schedule activities without violating a schedule constraint or delaying the project completion date. The late start dates are determined during the backward pass calculation of the project schedule network. (***PMBOK® Guide* – Third Edition**)

Latest Revised Estimate

SEE   Estimate at Completion (EAC)

(***PMBOK® Guide* – Third Edition**)

Layout Risk

The risk associated with the designed physical layout of a project. (***Const Ext***)

Lead [Technique]

A modification of a logical relationship that allows an acceleration of the successor activity. For example, in a finish-to-start dependency with a ten-day lead, the successor activity can start ten days before the predecessor activity has finished. A negative lead is equivalent to a positive lag. (***PMBOK® Guide* – Third Edition**)

SEE ALSO   Lag (***PMBOK® Guide* – Third Edition**)

Lessons Learned [Output/Input]

The learning gained from the process of performing the project. Lessons learned may be identified at any point. Also considered a project record, to be included in the lessons learned knowledge base. (***PMBOK® Guide* – Third Edition**)

Lessons Learned Knowledge Base

A store of historical information and lessons learned about both the outcomes of previous project selection decisions and previous project performance. (*PMBOK® Guide* – **Third Edition**)

Level of Effort (LOE)

1) Support-type *activity* (e.g., *seller* or *customer* liaison, project cost accounting, project management, etc.), which does not produce definitive end *products*. It is generally characterized by a uniform rate of *work* performance over a period of time determined by the activities supported. (*PMBOK® Guide* – **Third Edition**)(*PS-WBS*)

2) Support-type activity (e.g., seller or customer liaison, project cost accounting, project management), which does not produce definitive end products. (Note: The *PMBOK® Guide* – Third Edition definition for this term is broader and more inclusive in that it applies beyond the scope of the *Practice Standard for Earned Value Management*.) (*PS-EVM*)

Leveling

SEE   Resource Leveling (*PMBOK® Guide* – **Third Edition**)

Life Cycle

SEE   Project Life Cycle (*PMBOK® Guide* – **Third Edition**)

Line-Item Projects

Projects that are added to the budget of the government body on a project-by-project basis rather than as a program. (*Gov't Ext*)

SEE ALSO   Appropriation (*Gov't Ext*)
COMPARE TO Program (*Gov't Ext*)

Local Government

A government body of a small geographic region within a nation. Local governments may or may not overlap geographically. When local governments overlap, they typically have differing duties. Examples of local governments include counties, cities, towns, municipalities, school boards, water boards, road boards, sanitation districts, electrification districts, fire protection districts, and hospital districts. (*Gov't Ext*)

Log

A document used to record and describe or denote selected items identified during execution of a process or activity. Usually used with a modifier, such as issue, quality control, action, or defect. (*PMBOK® Guide* – **Third Edition**)

Logic

SEE   Network Logic (*PMBOK® Guide* – **Third Edition**)

Logic Diagram

SEE   Project Schedule Network Diagram
(*PMBOK® Guide* – **Third Edition**)

Logical Relationship

A dependency between two project schedule activities, or between a project schedule activity and a schedule milestone. The four possible types of logical relationships are: Finish-to-Start; Finish-to-Finish; Start-to-Start; and Start-to-Finish. (*PMBOK® Guide* – **Third Edition**)

SEE ALSO   Precedence Relationship
(*PMBOK® Guide* – **Third Edition**)

Lowest Responsible Seller

A responsible seller who submits the lowest bid or proposal that is responsive to the IFB or RFP, respectively. The selection process includes evaluation of each seller's proposal to ensure that it meets minimum qualifications of the government body. The degree of qualification may vary, but a seller must meet the minimum qualifications of the government body to be determined to be "responsible." For example, in construction contracts, the minimum qualifications are generally a contractor's license and a performance bond. For professional service contracts, a different selection process is used (*Gov't Ext*)

SEE ALSO   Responsible Seller (*Gov't Ext*)
COMPARE TO Qualifications-Based Selection (*Gov't Ext*)

Manage Project Team [Process]

The process of tracking team member performance, providing feedback, resolving issues, and coordinating changes to enhance project performance. (*PMBOK® Guide* – **Third Edition**)

Manage Stakeholders [Process]

The process of managing communications to satisfy the requirements of, and resolve issues with, project stakeholders. (*PMBOK® Guide* – **Third Edition**)

Management by Exception

A management technique that emphasizes attention to performance behavior that falls outside of some predetermined range of normal or expected outcomes. This technique is characterized by containment and conservatism. (*PS-EVM*)

Combined Standards Glossary
©2007 Project Management Institute, Four Campus Boulevard, Newtown Square, PA 19073-3299 USA

Management-by-Projects

The application of the project management discipline to achieve or extend an organization's strategic goals. (*Portfolio Management*)

Master Schedule [Tool]

A summary-level project schedule that identifies the major deliverables and work breakdown structure components and key schedule milestones. (*PMBOK® Guide* – **Third Edition**)

SEE ALSO   Milestone Schedule
(*PMBOK® Guide* – **Third Edition**)

Matching Funds

A form of split funding by program. When governments "devolve" project selection to lower representative bodies, they often require those lower bodies to pay a portion of the project cost. Matching funds may be apportioned on a percentage basis or as a defined contribution. (*Gov't Ext*)

SEE ALSO   Split Funding (*Gov't Ext*)
Defined Contribution (*Gov't Ext*)
Elements of Work (*Gov't Ext*)

Materiel

The aggregate of things used by an organization in any undertaking, such as equipment, apparatus, tools, machinery, gear, material, and supplies. (*PMBOK® Guide* – **Third Edition**)

Matrix Organization

Any organizational structure in which the project manager shares responsibility with the functional managers for assigning priorities and for directing the work of persons assigned to the project. (*PMBOK® Guide* – **Third Edition**)

Maturity State

An organization's degree of maturity in organizational project management. (*OPM3*)

Mechanism

A means used to perform a process. (*Portfolio Management*)

SEE ALSO   Technique (**Portfolio Management**)
SEE ALSO   Tool (**Portfolio Management**)

Methodology

A system of practices, techniques, procedures, and rules used by those who work in a discipline. (*PMBOK® Guide* – **Third Edition**)

Combined Standards Glossary
©2007 Project Management Institute, Four Campus Boulevard, Newtown Square, PA 19073-3299 USA

Milestone

A significant point or event in the project. (*PMBOK® Guide* – **Third Edition**)

> See Also   Schedule Milestone
> (*PMBOK® Guide* – **Third Edition**)

Milestone Schedule [Tool]

A summary-level schedule that identifies the major schedule milestones. (*PMBOK® Guide* – **Third Edition**)

> See Also   Master Schedule
> (*PMBOK® Guide* – **Third Edition**)

Monitor

Collect project performance data with respect to a plan, produce performance measures, and report and disseminate performance information. (*PMBOK® Guide* – **Third Edition**)

Monitor and Control Project Work [Process]

The process of monitoring and controlling the processes required to initiate, plan, execute, and close a project to meet the performance objectives defined in the project management plan and project scope statement. (*PMBOK® Guide* – **Third Edition**)

Monitoring

> See   Monitor (*PMBOK® Guide* – **Third Edition**)

Monitoring and Controlling Processes [Process Group]

1) Those processes performed to measure and monitor project execution so that corrective action can be taken when necessary to control the execution of the phase or project. (*PMBOK® Guide* – **Third Edition**)

2) Those processes performed to measure and monitor program execution so that corrective action can be taken when necessary to control the execution of the phase or program. (*Program Management*)

Monte Carlo Analysis

A technique that computes, or iterates, the project cost or project schedule many times using input values selected at random from probability distributions of possible costs or durations, to calculate a distribution of possible total project cost or completion dates. (*PMBOK® Guide* – **Third Edition**)

Motives

Things a person consistently thinks about or wants that cause action. Motives "drive and select" behavior toward certain action or goals and away from others. (*PMCDF*)

Multiple Award Schedules

A type of contract that can be used when there is a generally accepted "reasonable price" for a good or service. Multiple award schedules are particularly valuable for procurement of commodities. Each potential seller submits its qualifications and schedule of rates to the government body. Assuming each schedule of rates is based on generally accepted "reasonable" prices, the government body can select the seller that is most advantageous to the government. If these are approved, government agencies may buy goods and services at the published rates without a separate competition.(*Gov't Ext*)

Multi-Project Management

Those aspects of program management associated with initiating and coordinating the activities of multiple projects and the management of project managers. (*Program Management*)

National Government

The government of an internationally recognized nation. Examples of national governments include a confederation, federation, or unitary state. (*Gov't Ext*)

Near-Critical Activity

A schedule activity that has low total float. The concept of near-critical is equally applicable to a schedule activity or schedule network path. The limit below which total float is considered near critical is subject to expert judgment and varies from project to project. (*PMBOK® Guide – Third Edition*)

Network

SEE   Project Schedule Network Diagram
(*PMBOK® Guide – Third Edition*)

Network Analysis

SEE   Schedule Network Analysis
(*PMBOK® Guide – Third Edition*)

Network Logic

The collection of schedule activity dependencies that makes up a project schedule network diagram. (*PMBOK® Guide – Third Edition*)

Combined Standards Glossary
©2007 Project Management Institute, Four Campus Boulevard, Newtown Square, PA 19073-3299 USA

Network Loop

A schedule network path that passes the same node twice. Network loops cannot be analyzed using traditional schedule network analysis techniques such as critical path method. (*PMBOK® Guide* – **Third Edition**)

Network Open End

A schedule activity without any predecessor activities or successor activities creating an unintended break in a schedule network path. Network open ends are usually caused by missing logical relationships. (*PMBOK® Guide* – **Third Edition**)

Network Path

Any continuous series of schedule activities connected with logical relationships in a project schedule network diagram. (*PMBOK® Guide* – **Third Edition**)

Networking [Technique]

Developing relationships with persons who may be able to assist in the achievement of objectives and responsibilities. (*PMBOK® Guide* – **Third Edition**)

New Component

A component that is being added to an existing project portfolio. (*Portfolio Management*)

Node

One of the defining points of a schedule network; a junction point joined to some or all of the other dependency lines. (*PMBOK® Guide* – **Third Edition**)

> SEE ALSO Arrow Diagramming Method (ADM)
> (*PMBOK® Guide* – **Third Edition**)
> Precedence Diagramming Method (PDM)
> (*PMBOK® Guide* – **Third Edition**)

Non-Conformance Report

A report detailing the failure to meet specifications and often recommending a method of correction. (*Const Ext*)

Non-Recourse

A type of finance that relies on the project only as lending collateral. (*Const Ext*)

Objective

Something toward which work is to be directed, a strategic position to be attained, or a purpose to be achieved, a result to be obtained, a product to be produced, or a service to be performed. (*PMBOK® Guide* – **Third Edition**)

Obligation

A budget process that places funds for a contract into a separate account that can be used only for the specific contract. The funds remain available for two to five years, depending on the rules set by the representative body. This avoids the need to return to the government body and seek additional appropriation in each fiscal year. (*Gov't Ext*)

> See Also   Appropriation (*Gov't Ext*)
> Zero-Balance Budgeting (*Gov't Ext*)

On-Call Contracts

See   Indefinite Delivery Indefinite Quantity (IDIQ) Contracts (*Gov't Ext*)

Operational Management

Ongoing organizational activities associated with supporting functional elements, as opposed to project elements. Operational management also includes support of products that the organization has created through project activity. (*Program Management*)

Operations

An organizational function performing the ongoing execution of activities that produce the same product or provide a repetitive service. Examples are: production operations, manufacturing operations, and accounting operations. (*PMBOK® Guide* – **Third Edition**)

OPM3 Process Construct

The OPM3 Process Construct consists of all the components of OPM3, their dependencies and interrelationships, and how they are related to the three domains of organizational project management and to the four stages of process improvement. (*OPM3*)

Opportunity

A condition or situation favorable to the project, a positive set of circumstances, a positive set of events, a risk that will have a positive impact on project objectives, or a possibility for positive changes. Contrast with *threat*. (*PMBOK® Guide* – **Third Edition**)

Opposition Stakeholders

Stakeholders who perceive themselves as being harmed if the project is successful. (*Gov't Ext*)

Combined Standards Glossary
©2007 Project Management Institute, Four Campus Boulevard, Newtown Square, PA 19073-3299 USA

Organization

1) A group of persons organized for some purpose or to perform some type of work within an enterprise. (*PMBOK® Guide* – **Third Edition**)
2) Any company, agency, association, society, business unit, functional group, department, or sub-agency intending to make use of the OPM3 Standard. (*OPM3*)

Organization Chart [Tool]

A method for depicting interrelationships among a group of persons working together toward a common objective. (*PMBOK® Guide* – **Third Edition**)

Organizational Breakdown Structure (OBS) [Tool]

1) A hierarchically organized depiction of the project organization arranged so as to relate the work packages to the performing organizational units. (Sometimes OBS is written as Organization Breakdown Structure with the same definition.) (*PMBOK® Guide* – **Third Edition**)
2) A hierarchically organized depiction of the project organization arranged so as to relate the work to the performing organizational units. (Sometimes OBS is written as Organization Breakdown Structure with the same definition.) (Note: The *PMBOK® Guide* – Third Edition definition for this term is broader and more inclusive in that it applies beyond the scope of the *Practice Standard for Earned Value Management*.) (*PS-EVM*)
3) A hierarchically organized depiction of the project organization arranged so as to relate work packages to organizational units. (*PS-WBS*)

Organizational Governance

The process by which an organization directs and controls its operational and strategic activities, and by which the organization responds to the legitimate rights, expectations, and desires of its stakeholders. (*Portfolio Management*)

Organizational Process Assets [Output/Input]

Any or all process related assets, from any or all of the organizations involved in the project that are or can be used to influence the project's success. These process assets include formal and informal plans, policies, procedures, and guidelines. The process assets also include the organizations' knowledge bases such as lessons learned and historical information. (*PMBOK® Guide* – **Third Edition**)

Combined Standards Glossary
©2007 Project Management Institute, Four Campus Boulevard, Newtown Square, PA 19073-3299 USA

Organizational Project Management (OPM)

The application of knowledge, skills, tools, and techniques to organizational activities, as well as to project, program, and portfolio activities to achieve the aims of an organization through projects. (*OPM3*)

Organizational Project Management Maturity

The degree to which an organization practices organizational project management. In OPM3, this is reflected by the combination of Best Practices achieved within the Project, Program, and Portfolio domains. (*OPM3*)

Original Duration (OD)

The activity duration originally assigned to a schedule activity and not updated as progress is reported on the activity. Typically used for comparison with actual duration and remaining duration when reporting schedule progress. (*PMBOK® Guide* – **Third Edition**)

Other Than Full and Open Competition

A process where one or more responsible sources is excluded from competing for a contract. Examples of this scenario include a set-aside for small disadvantaged businesses or small and a sole source contract. (*Gov't Ext*)

> SEE ALSO   Sole Source Contract (*Gov't Ext*)

Other Work

Anything that fits into the "component definition" used by an organization and that cannot be classified as a business case, a project, a program, or a portfolio. (*Portfolio Management*)

Outcome

Outcome is the tangible or intangible result of applying a Capability. In the OPM3 framework, a Capability may have multiple Outcomes. The degree to which an Outcome is achieved is measured by a KPI (Key Performance Indicator). (*OPM3*)

Output [Process Output]

A product, result, or service generated by a process. May be an input to a successor process. (*PMBOK® Guide* – **Third Edition**)(*Program Management*)

Parametric Estimating [Technique]

An estimating technique that uses a statistical relationship between historical data and other variables (e.g., square footage in construction, lines of code in software development) to calculate an estimate for

Combined Standards Glossary
©2007 Project Management Institute, Four Campus Boulevard, Newtown Square, PA 19073-3299 USA

activity parameters, such as scope, cost, budget, and duration. This technique can produce higher levels of accuracy depending upon the sophistication and the underlying data built into the model. An example for the cost parameter is multiplying the planned quantity of work to be performed by the historical cost per unit to obtain the estimated cost. (***PMBOK® Guide*** – **Third Edition**)

Pareto Chart [Tool]

A histogram, ordered by frequency of occurrence, that shows how many results were generated by each identified cause. (***PMBOK® Guide*** **– Third Edition**)

Partnering (Alliance)

Alliance partnering is a long-term relationship between an owner and an engineer/contractor where the contractor acts as a part of the owner's organization for certain functions. (***Const Ext***)

Partnering (Project Specific)

An informal agreement of all major entities in a project to work closely and harmoniously together. (***Const Ext***)

Path Convergence

The merging or joining of parallel schedule network paths into the same node in a project schedule network diagram. Path convergence is characterized by a schedule activity with more than one predecessor activity. (***PMBOK® Guide*** – **Third Edition**)

Path Divergence

Extending or generating parallel schedule network paths from the same node in a project schedule network diagram. Path divergence is characterized by a schedule activity with more than one successor activity. (***PMBOK® Guide*** – **Third Edition**)

Percent Complete (PC or PCT)

An estimate, expressed as a percent, of the amount of work that has been completed on an activity or a work breakdown structure component. (***PMBOK® Guide*** – **Third Edition**)

Percentage Split

Split funding by program where each program funds a percentage of the project. (***Gov't Ext***)

Perform Quality Assurance (QA) [Process]

The process of applying the planned, systematic quality activities (such as audits or peer reviews) to ensure that the project employs all processes needed to meet requirements. (***PMBOK® Guide*** – **Third Edition**)

Perform Quality Control (QC) [Process]

The process of monitoring specific project results to determine whether they comply with relevant quality standards and identifying ways to eliminate causes of unsatisfactory performance. (*PMBOK® Guide – Third Edition*)

Performance Criteria

Refers to an integrated list of aspects of performance that would be regarded as displaying competent performance in the workplace in an Element of Competency. (*PMCDF*)

Performance Measurement Baseline (PMB)

1) An approved integrated *scope-schedule-cost** plan for the *project work* against which project execution is compared to measure and manage performance. Technical and *quality* parameters may also be included. (*PMBOK® Guide – Third Edition*)

2) An approved, integrated scope-schedule-cost plan for the project work against which project execution is compared to measure and manage performance. (Note: The *PMBOK® Guide – Third Edition* definition for this term is broader and more inclusive in that it applies beyond the scope of the *Practice Standard for Earned Value Management*.) (*PS-EVM*)

Performance Reporting [Process]

The process of collecting and distributing performance information. This includes status reporting, progress measurement, and forecasting. (*PMBOK® Guide – Third Edition*)

Performance Reports [Output/Input]

Documents and presentations that provide organized and summarized work performance information, earned value management parameters and calculations, and analyses of project work progress and status. Common formats for performance reports include bar charts, S-curves, histograms, tables, and project schedule network diagram showing current schedule status. (*PMBOK® Guide – Third Edition*)

Performing Organization

The enterprise whose personnel are most directly involved in doing the work of the project. (*PMBOK® Guide – Third Edition*)

Personal Data Assistant (PDA)

A portable handheld computerized device performing many communication and data storage functions. (*Const Ext*)

Personality

A unique organization of a relatively stable set of characteristics, tendencies, and temperaments that define an individual and determine that person's interaction with the environment. (*PMCDF*)

Phase

SEE   Project Phase (*PMBOK® Guide* – **Third Edition**) (*PS-WBS*)

Phase Gate

A review process at the end of a program phase where an oversight group, such as a program board or steering committee, decides to continue, continue with modification, or stop a program. (***Program Management***)

Phase Gates

Decision points for "go/no go" control decisions for projects, programs, and portfolios. (***Portfolio Management***)

Physical Work Progress

The amount of work physically completed on the project or task. This may be different from the amount of effort or money expended on the project or task. Predetermined techniques of claiming physical work progress that were selected during project planning are used to credit Earned Value when work is partially complete at the time of progress reporting. (*PS-EVM*)

Plan Contracting [Process]

The process of documenting the products, services, and results requirements and identifying potential sellers. (*PMBOK® Guide* – **Third Edition**)

Plan Purchases and Acquisitions [Process]

The process of determining what to purchase or acquire, and determining when and how to do so. (*PMBOK® Guide* – **Third Edition**)

Planned Finish Date (PF)

SEE   Scheduled Finish Date (SF)
      (*PMBOK® Guide* – **Third Edition**)

Planned Start Date (PS)

SEE Scheduled Start Date (SS)
      (*PMBOK® Guide* – **Third Edition**)

Planned Value (PV)

1)   The authorized budget assigned to the scheduled work to be accomplished for a schedule activity or work breakdown structure

component. Also referred to as the budgeted cost of work scheduled (BCWS). (*PMBOK® Guide* – **Third Edition**)

2) The authorized budget assigned to the scheduled work to be accomplished. Also referred to as the budgeted cost of work scheduled (BCWS). (Note: The *PMBOK® Guide* – Third Edition definition for this term is broader and more inclusive in that it applies beyond the scope of the *Practice Standard for Earned Value Management*.) (*PS-EVM*)

Planning Package

A WBS component below the control account with known work content but without detailed schedule activities. (*PMBOK® Guide* – **Third Edition**)

> See Also   Control Account (CA)
> (*PMBOK® Guide* – **Third Edition**)

Planning Processes [Process Group]

1) Those processes performed to define and mature the project scope, develop the project management plan, and identify and schedule the project activities that occur within the project. (*PMBOK® Guide* – **Third Edition**)

2) Those processes performed to define and mature the program scope, develop the management plan, and identify and schedule the activities that occur within the program. (*Program Management*)

Portfolio

1) A collection of projects or programs and other work that are grouped together to facilitate effective management of that work to meet strategic business objectives. The projects or programs of the portfolio may not necessarily be interdependent or directly related. (*PMBOK® Guide* – **Third Edition**)(*Portfolio Management*)(*PS-WBS*)

2) A Portfolio is a collection of projects and/or programs and other work grouped together to facilitate effective management of that work to meet strategic business objectives. The projects or programs of the Portfolio may not necessarily be interdependent or directly related. (*OPM3*)

Portfolio Balancing

The process of organizing the prioritized components into a component mix that has the best potential to collectively support and achieve strategic goals. (*Portfolio Management*)

Combined Standards Glossary
©2007 Project Management Institute, Four Campus Boulevard, Newtown Square, PA 19073-3299 USA

Portfolio Management [Technique]

1) The centralized management of one or more portfolios, which includes identifying, prioritizing, authorizing, managing, and controlling projects, programs, and other related work, to achieve specific strategic business objectives. (*PMBOK® Guide* – **Third Edition**)(*Portfolio Management*)(*PS-WBS*)

2) Portfolio Management refers to the selection and support of projects or program investments. These investments in projects and programs are guided by the organization's strategic plan and available resources. (*OPM3*)

Portfolio Management Communication Plan

A plan defining all communication needs, establishing communication requirements, specifying frequency, and identifying recipients for information associated with the portfolio management process. (*Portfolio Management*)

Portfolio Management Life Cycle

A life cycle of processes used to collect, identify, categorize, evaluate, select, prioritize, balance, authorize, and review components within the project portfolio to ensure that they are performing compared with the key indicators and the strategic plan. (*Portfolio Management*)

Portfolio Periodic Reporting and Review

The process of reporting on the portfolio components as a whole using key indicators and reviewing the performance of the component mix by comparing actual with anticipated evolution, value, risk level, spending, and strategic alignment. (*Portfolio Management*)

Position Description [Tool]

An explanation of a project team member's roles and responsibilities. (*PMBOK® Guide* – **Third Edition**)

Potential Component

A component that fits the predetermined "component definition," but has not yet been authorized to be part of the project portfolio. (*Portfolio Management*)

PPP

One of a group of categorizations in OPM3 to provide structure. It is used as a field in the Directories to indicate the three domains of Project, Program, and Portfolio Management. (*OPM3*)

Practice

A specific type of professional or management activity that contributes to the execution of a process and that may employ one or more techniques and tools. (*PMBOK® Guide* – **Third Edition**)

Precedence Diagramming Method (PDM) [Technique]

A schedule network diagramming technique in which schedule activities are represented by boxes (or nodes). Schedule activities are graphically linked by one or more logical relationships to show the sequence in which the activities are to be performed. (*PMBOK® Guide* – **Third Edition**)

Precedence Relationship

The term used in the precedence diagramming method for a logical relationship. In current usage, however, precedence relationship, logical relationship, and dependency are widely used interchangeably, regardless of the diagramming method used. (*PMBOK® Guide* – **Third Edition**)

Predecessor Activity

The schedule activity that determines when the logical successor activity can begin or end. (*PMBOK® Guide* – **Third Edition**)

Pre-Estimating Survey

A survey of a construction site to determine relevant characteristics such as weather, local suppliers and contractors and available utilities. (*Const Ext*)

Pre-Qualification List

A list of contractors or designers that have been pre-selected for further consideration based on their submitted qualifications. (*Const Ext*)

Prevailing Wage

The prevailing wage is often the wage paid to the largest number of people in the job classification in the geographic area. When so defined, the prevailing wage represents the "modal" average. However, the prevailing wage may also be defined as the "mean" average of the wages paid to all people in the job classification. (*Gov't Ext*)

Preventive Action

Documented direction to perform an activity that can reduce the probability of negative consequences associated with project risks. (*PMBOK® Guide* – **Third Edition**)

Combined Standards Glossary
©2007 Project Management Institute, Four Campus Boulevard, Newtown Square, PA 19073-3299 USA

Prioritization

The process of ranking the selected components based on their evaluation scores and other management considerations. (*Portfolio Management*)

Probability and Impact Matrix [Tool]

A common way to determine whether a risk is considered low, moderate, or high by combining the two dimensions of a risk: its probability of occurrence, and its impact on objectives if it occurs. (*PMBOK® Guide* – **Third Edition**)

Procedure

A series of steps followed in a regular definitive order to accomplish something. (*PMBOK® Guide* – **Third Edition**)

Process

A set of interrelated actions and activities performed to achieve a specified set of products, results, or services. (*PMBOK® Guide* – **Third Edition**)(*Program Management*)

Process Group

Same as the IPECC categorization as used in the *PMBOK® Guide*.

The Project Management process groups are as follows:
- Initiating Processes
- Planning Processes
- Executing Processes
- Controlling Processes
- Closing Processes (*OPM3*)
  SEE ALSO   Project Management Process Group (*PMBOK® Guide* – **Third Edition**)

Procurement Documents [Output/Input]

Those documents utilized in bid and proposal activities, which include buyer's Invitation for Bid, Invitation for Negotiations, Request for Information, Request for Quotation, Request for Proposal and seller's responses. (*PMBOK® Guide* – **Third Edition**)

Procurement Management Plan [Output/Input]

The document that describes how procurement processes from developing procurement documentation through contract closure will be managed. (*PMBOK® Guide* – **Third Edition**)

Product

An artifact that is produced, is quantifiable, and can be either an end item in itself or a component item. Additional words for products are materiel

Combined Standards Glossary
©2007 Project Management Institute, Four Campus Boulevard, Newtown Square, PA 19073-3299 USA

and goods. Contrast with *result* and *service*. (***PMBOK® Guide* – Third Edition**)

      SEE ALSO   Deliverable
                      (***PMBOK® Guide* – Third Edition**)

Product Life Cycle

A collection of generally sequential, non-overlapping product phases whose name and number are determined by the manufacturing and control needs of the organization. The last product life cycle phase for a product is generally the product's deterioration and death. Generally, a project life cycle is contained within one or more product life cycles. (***PMBOK® Guide* – Third Edition**)

Product Scope

The features and functions that characterize a product, service or result. (***PMBOK® Guide* – Third Edition**)(*PS-WBS*)

Product Scope Description

The documented narrative description of the product scope. (***PMBOK® Guide* – Third Edition**)

Program

1) A group of related projects managed in a coordinated way to obtain benefits and control not available from managing them individually. Programs may include elements of related work outside of the scope of the discrete projects in the program. (***PMBOK® Guide* – Third Edition**)(*OPM3*)(*Portfolio Management*)(*Program Management*)(*PS-WBS*)_

2) A group of projects managed in a coordinated way to obtain benefits not available by managing them individually. (***Gov't Ext***)

      SEE ALSO   Line Item Projects (***Gov't Ext***)

Program Governance

The process of developing, communicating, implementing, monitoring, and assuring the policies, procedures, organizational structures, and practices associated with a given program. (***Program Management***)

Program Management

1) The centralized coordinated management of a program to achieve the program's strategic objectives and benefits. (***PMBOK® Guide* – Third Edition**)(*Portfolio Management*)(*Program Management*)(*PS-WBS*)

2) The centralized, coordinated management of a program to achieve the program's strategic objectives and benefits. (***OPM3***)

Program Management Office (PMO)

The centralized management of a particular program or programs such that corporate benefit is realized by the sharing of resources, methodologies, tools, and techniques, and related high-level project management focus. (*PMBOK® Guide* – **Third Edition**)(*Portfolio Management*)

> SEE ALSO   Project Management Office (PMO) (*PMBOK® Guide* – **Third Edition**)

Program Management Process

Program management processes accomplish program management by receiving inputs and generating outputs, with the use of tools and techniques. In order to ensure that the outputs are delivered as required, the processes need to operate subject to controls. (*Program Management*)

Program Management Process Group

The process groups for program management comprise Initiating, Planning, Executing, Monitoring and Controlling, and Closing processes. (*Program Management*)

Program Stakeholders

Individuals and organizations that are actively involved in the program or whose interests may be positively or negatively affected by the program. (*Program Management*)

Progress Curves

Plots of (usually) progress in percent complete versus time. Used to display status and trends. (*Const Ext*)

Progressive Elaboration [Technique]

Continuously improving and detailing a plan as more detailed and specific information and more accurate estimates become available as the project progresses, and thereby producing more accurate and complete plans that result from the successive iterations of the planning process. (*PMBOK® Guide* – **Third Edition**)(*PS-WBS*)

Project

A temporary endeavor undertaken to create a unique product, service, or result. (*PMBOK® Guide* – **Third Edition**)(*OPM3*)(*Portfolio Management*)(*PS-WBS*)

Project Calendar

A calendar of working days or shifts that establishes those dates on which schedule activities are worked and nonworking days that determine those

Combined Standards Glossary
©2007 Project Management Institute, Four Campus Boulevard, Newtown Square, PA 19073-3299 USA

dates on which schedule activities are idle. Typically defines holidays, weekends and shift hours. (*PMBOK® Guide* – **Third Edition**)

       SEE ALSO   Resource Calendar
                    (*PMBOK® Guide* – **Third Edition**)

Project Charter [Output/Input]

A document issued by the project initiator or sponsor that formally authorizes the existence of a project, and provides the project manager with the authority to apply organizational resources to project activities. (*PMBOK® Guide* – **Third Edition**)

Project Communications Management [Knowledge Area]

Project Communications Management includes the processes required to ensure timely and appropriate generation, collection, distribution, storage, retrieval, and ultimate disposition of project information. The Project Communications Management processes provide the critical links among people and information that are necessary for successful communications. Project managers can spend an inordinate amount of time communicating with the project team, stakeholders, customer, and sponsor. Everyone involved in the project should understand how communications affect the project as a whole. Project Communications Management processes include communications planning, information distribution, performance reporting, and manage stakeholders. (*PMBOK® Guide* – **Third Edition**)

Project Cost Management [Knowledge Area]

Project Cost Management includes the processes involved in planning, estimating, budgeting, and controlling costs so that the project can be completed within the approved budget. The Project Cost Management processes include cost estimating, cost budgeting, and cost control. (*PMBOK® Guide* – **Third Edition**)

Project Human Resource Management [Knowledge Area]

Project Human Resource includes the processes that organize and manage the project team. The project team is comprised of the people who have assigned roles and responsibilities for completing the project. While it is common to speak of roles and responsibilities being assigned, team members should be involved in much of the project's planning and decision-making. Early involvement of team members adds expertise during the planning process and strengthens commitment to the project. The type and number of project team members can often change as the project progresses. Project team members can be referred to as the project's staff. Project Human Resource Management processes include human resource planning, acquire project team, develop project team, and manage project team. (*PMBOK® Guide* – **Third Edition**)

Combined Standards Glossary
©2007 Project Management Institute, Four Campus Boulevard, Newtown Square, PA 19073-3299 USA

Project Initiation

Launching a process that can result in the authorization and scope definition of a new project. (*PMBOK® Guide* – **Third Edition**)

Project Integration Management [Knowledge Area]

Project Integration Management includes the processes and activities needed to identify, define, combine, unify and coordinate the various processes and project management activities within the Project Management Process Groups. In the project management context, integration includes characteristics of unification, consolidation, articulation and integrative actions that are crucial to project completion, successfully meeting customer and stakeholder requirements and managing expectations. The Project Integration Management processes include develop project charter, develop preliminary project scope statement, develop project management plan, direct and manage project execution, monitor and control project work, integrated change control, and close project. (*PMBOK® Guide* – **Third Edition**)

Project Life Cycle

A collection of generally sequential project phases whose name and number are determined by the control needs of the organization or organizations involved in the project. A life cycle can be documented with a methodology. (*PMBOK® Guide* – **Third Edition**)

Project Management (PM)

The application of knowledge, skills, tools, and techniques to project activities to meet the project requirements. (*PMBOK® Guide* – **Third Edition**)(*OPM3*)(*Portfolio Management*)

Project Management Body of Knowledge

An inclusive term that describes the sum of knowledge within the profession of project management. As with other professions such as law, medicine, and accounting, the body of knowledge rests with the practitioners and academics that apply and advance it. The complete project management body of knowledge includes proven traditional practices that are widely applied and innovative practices that are emerging in the profession. The body of knowledge includes both published and unpublished material. The PMBOK is constantly evolving. (*PMBOK® Guide* – **Third Edition**)

Project Management Information System (PMIS) [Tool]

An information system consisting of the tools and techniques used to gather, integrate, and disseminate the outputs of project management processes. It is used to support all aspects of the project from initiating

Combined Standards Glossary
©2007 Project Management Institute, Four Campus Boulevard, Newtown Square, PA 19073-3299 USA

through closing, and can include both manual and automated systems. (*PMBOK® Guide* – **Third Edition**)

Project Management Knowledge Area

An identified area of project management defined by its knowledge requirements and described in terms of its component processes, practices, inputs, outputs, tools, and techniques. (*PMBOK® Guide* – **Third Edition**)

Project Management Office (PMO)

An organizational body or entity assigned various responsibilities related to the centralized and coordinated management of those projects under its domain. The responsibilities of a PMO can range from providing project management support functions to actually being responsible for the direct management of a project. (*PMBOK® Guide* – **Third Edition**)

SEE ALSO   Program Management Office (PMO)
(*PMBOK® Guide* – **Third Edition**)

Project Management Plan [Output/Input]

A formal, approved document that defines how the projected is executed, monitored and controlled. It may be summary or detailed and may be composed of one or more subsidiary management plans and other planning documents. (*PMBOK® Guide* – **Third Edition**)

Project Management Process

One of the 44 processes, unique to project management and described in the *PMBOK® Guide*. (*PMBOK® Guide* – **Third Edition**)

Project Management Process Group

1) A logical grouping of the project management processes described in the *PMBOK® Guide*. The project management process groups include Initiating Processes, Planning Processes, Executing Processes, Monitoring and Controlling Processes, and Closing Processes. Collectively, these five groups are required for any project, have clear internal dependencies, and must be performed in the same sequence on each project, independent of the application area or the specifics of the applied project life cycle. Project management process groups are not project phases. (*PMBOK® Guide* – **Third Edition**)

2) A logical grouping of the project management processes described in the *PMBOK® Guide*. The project management process groups include Initiating Processes, Planning Processes, Executing Processes, Monitoring and Controlling Processes, and Closing Processes. (*Program Management*)

Combined Standards Glossary
©2007 Project Management Institute, Four Campus Boulevard, Newtown Square, PA 19073-3299 USA

Project Management Professional (PMP®)

A person certified as a PMP® by the Project Management Institute (PMI®). (*PMBOK® Guide* – **Third Edition**)

Project Management Software [Tool]

A class of computer software applications specifically designed to aid the project management team with planning, monitoring, and controlling the project, including: cost estimating, scheduling, communications, collaboration, configuration management, document control, records management, and risk analysis. (*PMBOK® Guide* – **Third Edition**)

Project Management System [Tool]

The aggregation of the processes, tools, techniques, methodologies, resources, and procedures to manage a project. The system is documented in the project management plan and its content will vary depending upon the application area, organizational influence, complexity of the project, and the availability of existing systems. A project management system, which can be formal or informal, aids a project manager in effectively guiding a project to completion. A project management system is a set of processes and the related monitoring and control functions that are consolidated and combined into a functioning, unified whole. (*PMBOK® Guide* – **Third Edition**)

Project Management Team

The members of the project team who are directly involved in project management activities. On some smaller projects, the project management team may include virtually all of the project team members. (*PMBOK® Guide* – **Third Edition**)

Project Manager (PM)

The person assigned by the performing organization to achieve the project objectives. (*PMBOK® Guide* – **Third Edition**)

Project Organization Chart [Output/Input]

A document that graphically depicts the project team members and their interrelationships for a specific project. (*PMBOK® Guide* – **Third Edition**)

Project Performance

A measure of the extent to which the project is carried out as planned in terms of objectives, time, and financial constraints, and organizational policies and procedures. (*PMCDF*)

Project Phase

A collection of logically related project activities, usually culminating in the completion of a major deliverable. Project phases (also called phases) are mainly completed sequentially, but can overlap in some project situations. Phases can be subdivided into subphases and then components; this hierarchy, if the project or portions of the project are divided into phases, is contained in the work breakdown structure. A project phase is a component of a project life cycle. A project phase is not a project management process group. (*PMBOK® Guide* – **Third Edition**)(*PS-WBS*)

Project Process Groups

The five process groups required for any project that have clear dependencies and that are required to be performed in the same sequence on each project, independent of the application area or the specifics of the applied project life cycle. The process groups are initiating, planning, executing, monitoring and controlling, and closing. (*PMBOK® Guide* – **Third Edition**)

Project Procurement Management [Knowledge Area]

Project Procurement Management includes the processes to purchase or acquire the products, services, or results needed from outside the project team to perform the work. This chapter presents two perspectives of procurement. The organization can be either the buyer or seller of the product, service, or results under a contract.

Project Procurement Management includes the contract management and change control processes required to administer contracts or purchase orders issued by authorized project team members. Project Procurement Management also includes administering any contract issued by an outside organization (the buyer) that is acquiring the project from the performing organization (the seller) and administering contractual obligations placed on the project team by the contract. Project Procurement Management processes include plan purchases and acquisitions, plan contracting, request seller responses, select sellers, contract administration, and contract closure. (*PMBOK® Guide* – **Third Edition**)

Project Quality Management [Knowledge Area]

Project Quality Management includes the processes and activities of the performing organization that determine quality policies, objectives, and responsibilities so that the project will satisfy the needs for which it was undertaken. It implements the quality management system through policy and procedures, with continuous process improvement activities conducted throughout, as appropriate. The Project Quality Management processes include quality planning, perform quality assurance, and perform quality control. (*PMBOK® Guide* – **Third Edition**)

Combined Standards Glossary
©2007 Project Management Institute, Four Campus Boulevard, Newtown Square, PA 19073-3299 USA

Project Risk Management [Knowledge Area]

Project Risk Management includes the processes concerned with conducting risk management planning, identification, analysis, responses, and monitoring and control on a project. The objectives of Project Risk Management are to increase the probability and impact of positive events and decrease the probability and impact of events adverse to project objectives. Project Risk Management processes include risk management planning, risk identification, qualitative risk analysis, quantitative risk analysis, risk response planning, and risk monitoring and control. (*PMBOK® Guide* – **Third Edition**)

Project Schedule [Output/Input]

The planned dates for performing schedule activities and the planned dates for meeting schedule milestones. (*PMBOK® Guide* – **Third Edition**)

Project Schedule Network Diagram [Output/Input]

Any schematic display of the logical relationships among the project schedule activities. Always drawn from left to right to reflect project work chronology. (*PMBOK® Guide* – **Third Edition**)

Project Scope

The work that must be performed to deliver a product, service, or result with the specified features and functions. (*PMBOK® Guide* – **Third Edition**)(*PS-WBS*)

Project Scope Management [Knowledge Area]

Project Scope Management includes the processes required to ensure that the project includes all the work required, and only the work required, to complete the project successfully. Project Scope Management is primarily concerned with defining and controlling what is and is not included in the project. The Project Scope Management processes include scope planning, scope definition, create WBS, scope verification, and scope control. (*PMBOK® Guide* – **Third Edition**)

Project Scope Management Plan [Output/Input]

The document that describes how the project scope will be defined, developed, and verified and how the work breakdown structure will be created and defined, and that provides guidance on how the project scope will be managed and controlled by the project management team. It is contained in or is a subsidiary plan of the project management plan. The project scope management plan can be informal and broadly framed, or formal and highly detailed, based on the needs of the project. (*PMBOK® Guide* – **Third Edition**)

Combined Standards Glossary
©2007 Project Management Institute, Four Campus Boulevard, Newtown Square, PA 19073-3299 USA

Project Scope Statement [Output/Input]

The narrative description of the project scope, including major deliverables, project objectives, project assumptions, project constraints, and a statement of work, that provides a documented basis for making future project decisions and for confirming or developing a common understanding of project scope among the stakeholders. The definition of the project scope – what needs to be accomplished. (*PMBOK® Guide* – **Third Edition**)

Project Specifications

The engineering and architectural plans and written requirements for a project. Similar to statement of work. (*Const Ext*)

Project Sponsor

SEE   Sponsor (*PMBOK® Guide* – **Third Edition**)

Project Stakeholder

SEE   Stakeholder (*PMBOK® Guide* – **Third Edition**)

Project Success

For the purpose of this document, project success is defined as a collective assessment by project stakeholders (e.g., client/customer, sponsor) of the degree to which the project has achieved each of its objectives. (*PMCDF*)

Project Summary Work Breakdown Structure (PSWBS) [Tool]

A work breakdown structure for the project that is only developed down to the subproject level of detail within some legs of the WBS, and where the detail of those subprojects are provided by use of contract work breakdown structures. (*PMBOK® Guide* – **Third Edition**)

Project Team

All the project team members, including the project management team, the project manager and, for some projects, the project sponsor. (*PMBOK® Guide* – **Third Edition**)

Project Team Directory

A documented list of project team members, their project roles and communication information. (*PMBOK® Guide* – **Third Edition**)

Project Team Members

The persons who report either directly or indirectly to the project manager, and who are responsible for performing project work as a regular part of their assigned duties. (*PMBOK® Guide* – **Third Edition**)

Project Time Management [Knowledge Area]

Project Time Management includes the processes required to accomplish timely completion of the project. The Project Time Management processes include activity definition, activity sequencing, activity resource estimating, activity duration estimating, schedule development, and schedule control. (*PMBOK® Guide* – **Third Edition**)

Project Work

SEE   Work (*PMBOK® Guide* – **Third Edition**)

Projectized Organization

Any organizational structure in which the project manager has full authority to assign priorities, apply resources, and direct the work of persons assigned to the project. (*PMBOK® Guide* – **Third Edition**)

Protest

A formal objection to the selection or award of a government contract to a seller by a disappointed seller or any other person. The formal objection typically must be filed during the selection process and comply with a mandatory procedure established by the government body. (*Gov't Ext*)

Punchlist

The items remaining to be completed after a final inspection. (*Const Ext*)

Qualifications-Based Selection

A selection process in which the contract is awarded to the best-qualified seller among those who offer a reasonable price to the government. This approach is most often used on design contracts, where the design cost is a small fraction of the construction cost, but increased attention to design can result in large construction savings. Sellers' qualifications are evaluated, the sellers are ranked, and a contract is negotiated with the most qualified seller. If the government and the seller cannot agree on a reasonable price, the government terminates negotiations with the highest-ranked seller and begins negotiating with the next highest-ranked seller. (*Gov't Ext*)

Qualitative Risk Analysis [Process]

Performing a qualitative analysis of risks and conditions to prioritize their effects on project objectives. It involves assessing the probability and impact of project risk(s) and using methods such as the probability and impact matrix to classify risks into categories of high, moderate, and low for prioritized risk response planning. (*PMBOK® Guide* – **Third Edition**)

Combined Standards Glossary
©2007 Project Management Institute, Four Campus Boulevard, Newtown Square, PA 19073-3299 USA

Quality

The degree to which a set of inherent characteristics fulfills requirements. (*PMBOK® Guide* – **Third Edition**)

Quality Management Plan [Output/Input]

The quality management plan describes how the project management team will implement the performing organization's quality policy. The quality management plan is a component or a subsidiary plan of the project management plan. The quality management plan may be formal or informal, highly detailed, or broadly framed, based on the requirements of the project. (*PMBOK® Guide* – **Third Edition**)

Quality Planning [Process]

The process of identifying which quality standards are relevant to the project and determining how to satisfy them. (*PMBOK® Guide* – **Third Edition**)

Quantitative Risk Analysis [Process]

The process of numerically analyzing the effect on overall project objectives of identified risks. (*PMBOK® Guide* – **Third Edition**)

Recourse

Financing that is based on the assets of the sponsoring entity for collateral. (*Const Ext*)

Regional Government

A government body of a large region within a nation. In small nations, there are often no regional governments—only a national government and local governments. In confederations and federations, the regional government has considerable autonomy. In unitary states, the regional government is subject to control by the national government. Examples of regional governments include states, provinces, departments, cantons, kingdoms, principalities, republics, regions, and territories. (*Gov't Ext*)

Regulation

Requirements imposed by a governmental body. These requirements can establish product, process or service characteristics—including applicable administrative provisions—that have government-mandated compliance. (*PMBOK® Guide* – **Third Edition**)

Regulators

Individuals or organizations that must approve various aspects of the project. Regulators enforce rules and regulations. They are actively involved in the project, but generally have no interest in its success—it will not affect them. Regulators are either agents of a higher government

Combined Standards Glossary
©2007 Project Management Institute, Four Campus Boulevard, Newtown Square, PA 19073-3299 USA

or of another agency in the same government as the performing organization. (*Gov't Ext*)

Reliability

The probability of a product performing its intended function under specific conditions for a given period of time. (***PMBOK® Guide* – Third Edition**)

Remaining Duration (RD)

The time in calendar units, between the data date of the project schedule and the finish date of a schedule activity that has an actual start date. This represents the time needed to complete a schedule activity where the work is in progress. (***PMBOK® Guide* – Third Edition**)

Representative Body

A group of people, elected by the voters, who meet, deliberate, and set rules. They may call these rules by several names. They include laws, statutes, ordinances, regulations, and policies. (*Gov't Ext*)

Resource Breakdown Structure (RBS)

A hierarchical structure of resources by resource category and resource type used in resource leveling schedules and to develop resource-limited schedules, and which may be used to identify and analyze *project* human resource assignments. (*PS-WBS*)

Responsible Seller

A seller that meets the minimum qualifications required by the government body to perform the work. (*Gov't Ext*)

Request for Information (RFI)

1) A type of procurement document whereby the buyer requests a potential seller to provide various pieces of information related to a product or service or seller capability. (***PMBOK® Guide* – Third Edition**)
2) Typically a communication from a contractor to the designer. (*Const Ext*)

Request for Proposal (RFP)

A type of procurement document used to request proposals from prospective sellers of products or services. In some application areas, it may have a narrower or more specific meaning. (***PMBOK® Guide* – Third Edition**)

Request for Quotation (RFQ)

A type of procurement document used to request price quotations from prospective sellers of common or standard products or services. Sometimes used in place of request for proposal and in some application areas, it may have a narrower or more specific meaning. (*PMBOK® Guide* – Third Edition)

Request Seller Responses [Process]
The process of obtaining information, quotations, bids, offers, or proposals, as appropriate. (*PMBOK® Guide* – Third Edition)

Requested Change [Output/Input]
A formally documented change request that is submitted for approval to the integrated change control process. Contrast with *approved change request*. (*PMBOK® Guide* – Third Edition)

Requirement
A condition or capability that must be met or possessed by a system, product, service, result, or component to satisfy a contract, standard, specification, or other formally imposed documents. Requirements include the quantified and documented needs, wants, and expectations of the sponsor, customer, and other stakeholders. (*PMBOK® Guide* – Third Edition)

Reserve
A provision in the project management plan to mitigate cost and/or schedule risk. Often used with a modifier (e.g., management reserve, contingency reserve) to provide further detail on what types of risk are meant to be mitigated. The specific meaning of the modified term varies by application area. (*PMBOK® Guide* – Third Edition)

Reserve Analysis [Technique]
An analytical technique to determine the essential features and relationships of components in the project management plan to establish a reserve for the schedule duration, budget, estimated cost, or funds for a project. (*PMBOK® Guide* – Third Edition)

Residual Risk
A risk that remains after risk responses have been implemented. (*PMBOK® Guide* – Third Edition)

Resource
Skilled human resources (specific disciplines either individually or in crews or teams), equipment, services, supplies, commodities, materiel, budgets, or funds. (*PMBOK® Guide* – Third Edition)

Resource Breakdown Structure (RBS)
A hierarchical structure of resources by resource category and resource type used in resource leveling schedules and to develop resource-limited schedules, and which may be used to identify and analyze project human resource assignments. (*PMBOK® Guide* – Third Edition)(*PS-WBS*)

Resource Calendar

A calendar of working days and nonworking days that determines those dates on which each specific resource is idle or can be active. Typically defines resource specific holidays and resource availability periods. (*PMBOK® Guide* – **Third Edition**)

> SEE ALSO   Project Calendar
> (*PMBOK® Guide* – **Third Edition**)

Resource-Constrained Schedule

> SEE   Resource-Limited Schedule
> (*PMBOK® Guide* – **Third Edition**)

Resource Histogram

A bar chart showing the amount of time that a resource is scheduled to work over a series of time periods. Resource availability may be depicted as a line for comparison purposes. Contrasting bars may show actual amounts of resource used as the project progresses. (*PMBOK® Guide* – **Third Edition**)

Resource Leveling [Technique]

Any form of schedule network analysis in which scheduling decisions (start and finish dates) are driven by resource constraints (e.g., limited resource availability or difficult-to-manage changes in resource availability levels). (*PMBOK® Guide* – **Third Edition**)

Resource-Limited Schedule

A project schedule whose schedule activity, scheduled start dates and scheduled finish dates reflect expected resource availability. A resource-limited schedule does not have any early or late start or finish dates. The resource-limited schedule total float is determined by calculating the difference between the critical path method late finish date and the resource-limited scheduled finish date. Sometimes called resource-constrained schedule. (*PMBOK® Guide* – **Third Edition**)

> SEE ALSO   Resource Leveling
> (*PMBOK® Guide* – **Third Edition**)

Resource Planning

> SEE   Activity Resource Estimating
> (*PMBOK® Guide* – **Third Edition**)

Responsibility Assignment Matrix (RAM) [Tool]

A structure that relates the project *organizational breakdown structure* to the *work breakdown structure* to help ensure that each component of the project's *scope* of *work* is assigned to a responsible person/team. (*PMBOK® Guide* – **Third Edition**) (*PS-EVM*)

Combined Standards Glossary
©2007 Project Management Institute, Four Campus Boulevard, Newtown Square, PA 19073-3299 USA

Result

An output from performing project management processes and activities. Results include outcomes (e.g., integrated systems, revised process, restructured organization, tests, trained personnel, etc.) and documents (e.g., policies, plans, studies, procedures, specifications, reports, etc.). Contrast with *product* and *service*. (*PMBOK® Guide* – Third Edition)

SEE ALSO   Deliverable
(*PMBOK® Guide* – Third Edition)

Retainage

A portion of a contract payment that is withheld until contract completion to ensure full performance of the contract terms. (*PMBOK® Guide* – Third Edition)

Rework

Action taken to bring a defective or nonconforming component into compliance with requirements or specifications. (*PMBOK® Guide* – Third Edition)

Risk

An uncertain event or condition that, if it occurs, has a positive or negative effect on a project's objectives. (*PMBOK® Guide* – Third Edition)(*PS-WBS*)

SEE ALSO   Risk Breakdown Structure (RBS)
(*PMBOK® Guide* – Third Edition)
Risk Category (*PMBOK® Guide* – Third Edition)

Risk Acceptance [Technique]

A risk response planning technique that indicates that the project team has decided not to change the project management plan to deal with a risk, or is unable to identify any other suitable response strategy. (*PMBOK® Guide* – Third Edition)

Risk Avoidance [Technique]

A risk response planning technique for a threat that creates changes to the project management plan that are meant to either eliminate the risk or to protect the project objectives from its impact. Generally, risk avoidance involves relaxing the time, cost, scope, or quality objectives. (*PMBOK® Guide* – Third Edition)

Risk Breakdown Structure (RBS) [Tool]

A hierarchically organized depiction of the identified project risks arranged by risk category and subcategory that identifies the various areas and causes of potential risks. The risk breakdown structure is often tailored to specific project types. (*PMBOK® Guide* – Third Edition)

Combined Standards Glossary
©2007 Project Management Institute, Four Campus Boulevard, Newtown Square, PA 19073-3299 USA

Risk Category

A group of potential causes of risk. Risk causes may be grouped into categories such as technical, external, organizational, environmental, or project management. A category may include subcategories such as technical maturity, weather, or aggressive estimating. (*PMBOK® Guide –* **Third Edition)**

SEE ALSO   Risk Breakdown Structure (RBS)
(*PMBOK® Guide* – **Third Edition)**

Risk Database

A repository that provides for collection, maintenance, and analysis of data gathered and used in the risk management processes. (*PMBOK® Guide* – **Third Edition)**

Risk Event

A discrete occurrence that may affect the project for better or worse. (*PS-WBS*)

Risk Identification [Process]

The process of determining which risks might affect the project and documenting their characteristics. (*PMBOK® Guide* – **Third Edition)**

Risk Management Plan [Output/Input]

The document describing how project risk management will be structured and performed on the project. It is contained in or is a subsidiary plan of the project management plan. The risk management plan can be informal and broadly framed, or formal and highly detailed, based on the needs of the project. Information in the risk management plan varies by application area and project size. The risk management plan is different from the risk register that contains the list of project risks, the results of risk analysis, and the risk responses. (*PMBOK® Guide* – **Third Edition)**

Risk Management Planning [Process]

The process of deciding how to approach, plan, and execute risk management activities for a project. (*PMBOK® Guide* – **Third Edition)**

Risk Mitigation [Technique]

A risk response planning technique associated with threats that seeks to reduce the probability of occurrence or impact of a risk to below an acceptable threshold. (*PMBOK® Guide* – **Third Edition)**

Risk Monitoring and Control [Process]

The process of tracking identified risks, monitoring residual risks, identifying new risks, executing risk response plans, and evaluating their effectiveness throughout the project life cycle. (*PMBOK® Guide* – **Third Edition)**

Combined Standards Glossary
©2007 Project Management Institute, Four Campus Boulevard, Newtown Square, PA 19073-3299 USA

Risk Register [Output/Input]

The document containing the results of the qualitative risk analysis, quantitative risk analysis, and risk response planning. The risk register details all identified risks, including description, category, cause, probability of occurring, impact(s) on objectives, proposed responses, owners, and current status. The risk register is a component of the project management plan. (*PMBOK® Guide* – **Third Edition**)

Risk Response Planning [Process]

The process of developing options and actions to enhance opportunities and to reduce threats to project objectives. (*PMBOK® Guide* – **Third Edition**)

Risk Transference [Technique]

A risk response planning technique that shifts the impact of a threat to a third party, together with ownership of the response. (*PMBOK® Guide* – **Third Edition**)

Role

A defined function to be performed by a project team member, such as testing, filing, inspecting, coding. (*PMBOK® Guide* – **Third Edition**)

Rolling Wave Planning [Technique]

A form of progressive elaboration planning where the work to be accomplished in the near term is planned in detail at a low level of the work breakdown structure, while the work far in the future is planned at a relatively high level of the work breakdown structure, but the detailed planning of the work to be performed within another one or two periods in the near future is done as work is being completed during the current period. (*PMBOK® Guide* – **Third Edition**)

Root Cause Analysis [Technique]

An analytical technique used to determine the basic underlying reason that causes a variance or a defect or a risk. A root cause may underlie more than one variance or defect or risk. (*PMBOK® Guide* – **Third Edition**)

S-Curve

1) Graphic display of cumulative *costs*, labor hours, percentage of *work*, or other quantities, plotted against time. Used to depict *planned value*, *earned value*, and *actual cost* of project work. The name derives from the S-like shape of the curve (flatter at the beginning and end, steeper in the middle) produced on a *project* that starts slowly, accelerates, and then tails off. Also a term for the cumulative likelihood distribution that is a *result* of a *simulation*,

Combined Standards Glossary
©2007 Project Management Institute, Four Campus Boulevard, Newtown Square, PA 19073-3299 USA

a *tool* of *quantitative risk analysis*. (*PMBOK® Guide* – **Third Edition**)

2) Graphic display of cumulative costs, labor hours, percentage of work, or other quantities, plotted against time. Used to depict Planned Value, Earned Value, and Actual Cost of project work. (Note: The *PMBOK® Guide* – Third Edition definition for this term is broader and more inclusive in that it applies beyond the scope of the *Practice Standard for Earned Value Management*.) (***PS-EVM***)

SAP

A business services and application software firm providing accounting software among other products. (***Const Ext***)

Schedule

SEE   Project Schedule (*PMBOK® Guide* – **Third Edition**)
Schedule Model (*PMBOK® Guide* – **Third Edition**)

Schedule Activity

A discrete scheduled component of work performed during the course of a project. A schedule activity normally has an estimated duration, an estimated cost, and estimated resource requirements. Schedule activities are connected to other schedule activities or schedule milestones with logical relationships, and are decomposed from work packages. (*PMBOK® Guide* – **Third Edition**)

Schedule Analysis

SEE   Schedule Network Analysis
(*PMBOK® Guide* – **Third Edition**)

Schedule Compression [Technique]

Shortening the project schedule duration without reducing the project scope. (*PMBOK® Guide* – **Third Edition**)
SEE ALSO   Crashing (*PMBOK® Guide* – **Third Edition**)
Fast Tracking
(*PMBOK® Guide* – **Third Edition**)

Schedule Control [Process]

The process of controlling changes to the project schedule. (*PMBOK® Guide* – **Third Edition**)

Schedule Development [Process]

The process of analyzing schedule activity sequences, schedule activity durations, resource requirements, and schedule constraints to create the project schedule. (*PMBOK® Guide* – **Third Edition**)

Combined Standards Glossary
©2007 Project Management Institute, Four Campus Boulevard, Newtown Square, PA 19073-3299 USA

Schedule Management Plan [Output/Input]

The document that establishes criteria and the activities for developing and controlling the project schedule. It is contained in, or is a subsidiary plan of, the project management plan. The schedule management plan may be formal or informal, highly detailed or broadly framed, based on the needs of the project. (*PMBOK® Guide* – **Third Edition**)

Schedule Milestone

A significant event in the project schedule, such as an event restraining future work or marking the completion of a major deliverable. A schedule milestone has zero duration. Sometimes called a milestone activity. (*PMBOK® Guide* – **Third Edition**)

> SEE ALSO   Milestone (*PMBOK® Guide* – **Third Edition**)

Schedule Model [Tool]

A model used in conjunction with manual methods or project management software to perform schedule network analysis to generate the project schedule for use in managing the execution of a project. (*PMBOK® Guide* – **Third Edition**)

> SEE ALSO   Project Schedule
> (*PMBOK® Guide* – **Third Edition**)

Schedule Network Analysis [Technique]

The technique of identifying early and late start dates, as well as early and late finish dates, for the uncompleted portions of project schedule activities. (*PMBOK® Guide* – **Third Edition**)

> SEE ALSO   Critical Chain Method
> (*PMBOK® Guide* – **Third Edition**)
> Critical Path Method
> (*PMBOK® Guide* – **Third Edition**)
> Resource Leveling
> (*PMBOK® Guide* – **Third Edition**)

Schedule Performance Index (SPI)

A measure of schedule efficiency on a project. It is the ratio of earned value (EV) to planned value (PV). The SPI = EV divided by PV. An SPI equal to or greater than one indicates a favorable condition and a value of less than one indicates an unfavorable condition. (*PMBOK® Guide* – **Third Edition**) (*PS-EVM*)

> SEE ALSO   Earned Value Management (EVM)
> (*PMBOK® Guide* – **Third Edition**)

Schedule Variance (SV)

1) A measure of schedule performance on a project. It is the algebraic difference between the earned value (EV) and the planned value (PV). SV = EV minus PV. (*PMBOK® Guide* – **Third Edition**)
2) A measure of schedule performance on a project. It is the algebraic difference between the earned value (EV) and the planned value (PV). SV = EV minus PV. (Note: The *PMBOK® Guide* – Third Edition definition for this term is broader and more inclusive in that it applies beyond the scope of the *Practice Standard for Earned Value Management*). (*PS-EVM*)

      SEE ALSO   Earned Value Management (EVM)
      (*PMBOK® Guide* – **Third Edition**)

Scheduled Finish Date (SF)

The point in time that work was scheduled to finish on a schedule activity. The scheduled finish date is normally within the range of dates delimited by the early finish date and the late finish date. It may reflect resource leveling of scarce resources. Sometimes called planned finish date. (*PMBOK® Guide* – **Third Edition**)

Scheduled Start Date (SS)

The point in time that work was scheduled to start on a schedule activity. The scheduled start date is normally within the range of dates delimited by the early start date and the late start date. It may reflect resource leveling of scarce resources. Sometimes called planned start date. (*PMBOK® Guide* – **Third Edition**)

Scope

The sum of the products, services, and results to be provided as a project. (*PMBOK® Guide* – **Third Edition**) (*PS-WBS*)

      SEE ALSO   Product Scope
      (*PMBOK® Guide* – **Third Edition**)
      Project Scope
      (*PMBOK® Guide* – **Third Edition**)

Scope Baseline

      SEE   Baseline (*PMBOK® Guide* – **Third Edition**)

Scope Change

Any change to the project scope. A scope change almost always requires an adjustment to the project cost or schedule. (*PMBOK® Guide* – **Third Edition**) (*PS-WBS*)

Scope Control [Process]

The process of controlling changes to the project scope. (*PMBOK® Guide* – **Third Edition**)

Combined Standards Glossary
©2007 Project Management Institute, Four Campus Boulevard, Newtown Square, PA 19073-3299 USA

Scope Creep

Adding features and functionality (project scope) without addressing the effects on time, costs, and resources, or without customer approval. (*PMBOK® Guide* – **Third Edition**)

Scope Definition [Process]

The process of developing a detailed project scope statement as the basis for future project decisions. (*PMBOK® Guide* – **Third Edition**)

Scope Planning [Process]

The process of creating a project scope management plan. (*PMBOK® Guide* – **Third Edition**)

Scope Verification [Process]

The process of formalizing acceptance of the completed project deliverables. (*PMBOK® Guide* – **Third Edition**)

Scoring Model

A set of weighted criteria and corresponding key indicators to measure and score components for comparison and prioritization purposes. (*Portfolio Management*)

Secondary Risk

A risk that arises as a direct result of implementing a risk response. (*PMBOK® Guide* – **Third Edition**)

Selection

The process of deciding on the components to be put forward from evaluation to prioritization based on their evaluation scores. (*Portfolio Management*)

Select Sellers [Process]

The process of reviewing offers, choosing from among potential sellers, and negotiating a written contract with a seller. (*PMBOK® Guide* – **Third Edition**)

Self-Concept

View of oneself, often different from the view others hold of the individual. (*PMCDF*)

Self-Performed

Construction work that is performed by the major contractor's work force. (*Const Ext*)

Seller

A provider or supplier of products, services, or results to an organization. (*PMBOK® Guide* – **Third Edition**)

Sensitivity Analysis

1) A quantitative risk analysis and modeling technique used to help determine which risks have the most potential impact on the project. It examines the extent to which the uncertainty of each project element affects the objective being examined when all other uncertain elements are held at their baseline values. The typical display of results is in the form of a tornado diagram. (*PMBOK® Guide* – **Third Edition**)

2) Varying several constituents of a calculated study to see what the effect is. Usually performed in connection with a feasibility study. (*Const Ext*)

Service

Useful work performed that does not produce a tangible product or result, such as performing any of the business functions supporting production or distribution. Contrast with *product* and *result*. (*PMBOK® Guide* – **Third Edition**)

> SEE ALSO   Deliverable
> (*PMBOK® Guide* – **Third Edition**)

Short List

A list that is distilled from a larger group of proposers or bidders through the use of set criteria. (*Const Ext*)

Should-Cost Estimate

An estimate of the cost of a product or service used to provide an assessment of the reasonableness of a prospective seller's proposed cost. (*PMBOK® Guide* – **Third Edition**)

Simulation

A simulation uses a project model that translates the uncertainties specified at a detailed level into their potential impact on objectives that are expressed at the level of the total project. Project simulations use computer models and estimates of risk, usually expressed as a probability distribution of possible costs or durations at a detailed work level, and are typically performed using Monte Carlo analysis. (*PMBOK® Guide* – **Third Edition**)

Skill

1) Ability to use knowledge, a developed aptitude, and/or a capability to effectively and readily execute or perform an activity. (*PMBOK® Guide* – **Third Edition**)

2) Proficiency, facility, or dexterity that is acquired or developed through training or experience; an art, trade or technique, requiring the use of the hands, body, or mind. (*PMCDF*)

Combined Standards Glossary
©2007 Project Management Institute, Four Campus Boulevard, Newtown Square, PA 19073-3299 USA

Slack

SEE   Free Float (FF) (***PMBOK® Guide* – Third Edition**)
Total Float (TF) (***PMBOK® Guide* – Third Edition**)

SMCI

One of three categorizations used to provide a framework for the OPM3 (PPP, SMCI, IPECC). SMCI is an acronym for the four Process Improvement Stages: Standardize, Measure, Control, and Improve. (***OPM3***)

Sole Source

A type of procurement where only one supplier is asked to bid. Often required to obtain proprietary products. (***Const Ext***)

Sole Source Contract

A contract in which there is only a single seller that can accomplish the work—by reason of experience, possession of specialized facilities, or technical competence—in a time frame required by the government.

SEE ALSO   Other Than Full and Open Competition (***Gov't Ext***)

Special Cause

A source of variation that is not inherent in the system, is not predictable, and is intermittent. It can be assigned to a defect in the system. On a control chart, points beyond the control limits, or non-random patterns within the control limits, indicate it. Also referred to as assignable cause. Contrast with *common cause*. (***PMBOK® Guide* – Third Edition**)

Specification

A document that specifies, in a complete, precise, verifiable manner, the requirements, design, behavior, or other characteristics of a system, component, product, result, or service and, often, the procedures for determining whether these provisions have been satisfied. Examples are: requirement specification, design specification, product specification, and test specification. (***PMBOK® Guide* – Third Edition**)

Specification Limits

The area, on either side of the centerline, or mean, of data plotted on a control chart that meets the customer's requirements for a product or service. This area may be greater than or less than the area defined by the control limits. (***PMBOK® Guide* – Third Edition**)

SEE ALSO   Control Limits
(***PMBOK® Guide* – Third Edition**)

Split Funding

A project that receives funding from multiple fund sources or from budgets in more than one budget year. (*Gov't Ext*)

> SEE ALSO   Matching Funds (*Gov't Ext*)
> Defined Contribution (*Gov't Ext*)
> Defined Elements of Work (*Gov't Ext*)

Spoils System

A system in which each new administration can replace government employees. (*Gov't Ext*)

> SEE ALSO   Civil Service System (*Gov't Ext*)

Sponsor

1) The person or group that provides the financial resources, in cash or in kind, for the project. (*PMBOK® Guide* – **Third Edition**)
2) The person or group that provides the financial resources, in cash or in-kind, for the program. (*Program Management*)

Staffing Management Plan [Process]

The document that describes when and how human resource requirements will be met. It is contained in, or is a subsidiary plan of, the project management plan. The staffing management plan can be informal and broadly framed, or formal and highly detailed, based on the needs of the project. Information in the staffing management plan varies by application area and project size. (*PMBOK® Guide* – **Third Edition**)

Stakeholder

1) Persons and organizations such as customers, sponsors, performing organization and the public, that are actively involved in the project, or whose interests may be positively or negatively affected by execution or completion of the project. They may also exert influence over the project and its deliverables. (*PMBOK® Guide* – **Third Edition**)
2) Person or organization (e.g., customer, sponsor, performing organization, or the public) that is actively involved in the project, or whose interests may be positively or negatively affected by execution or completion of the project. A stakeholder may also exert influence over the project and its deliverables. (*PS-WBS*)

Standard

A document established by consensus and approved by a recognized body that provides, for common and repeated use, rules, guidelines or characteristics for activities or their results, aimed at the achievement of

©2007 Project Management Institute, Four Campus Boulevard, Newtown Square, PA 19073-3299 USA

the optimum degree of order in a given context. (*PMBOK® Guide –* **Third Edition**)(*PS-WBS*)

Start Date

A point in time associated with a schedule activity's start, usually qualified by one of the following: actual, planned, estimated, scheduled, early, late, target, baseline, or current. (*PMBOK® Guide –* **Third Edition**)

Start-to-Finish (SF)

The logical relationship where completion of the successor schedule activity is dependent upon the initiation of the predecessor schedule activity. (*PMBOK® Guide –* **Third Edition**)

      SEE ALSO   Logical Relationship
                       (*PMBOK® Guide –* **Third Edition**)

Start-to-Start (SS)

The logical relationship where initiation of the work of the successor schedule activity depends upon the initiation of the work of the predecessor schedule activity. (*PMBOK® Guide –* **Third Edition**)

      SEE ALSO   Logical Relationship
                       (*PMBOK® Guide –* **Third Edition**)

Statement of Work (SOW)

A narrative description of products, services, or results to be supplied. (*PMBOK® Guide –* **Third Edition**)(*PS-WBS*)

Steering Committee

The group responsible for ensuring program goals are achieved and providing support to address program risks and issues. Sometimes this group is known as a Program Board or Governance Board. (*Program Management*)

Strategic Change

Any change in the strategic intentions and plans of the organization that can impact the contents of component definition, categories, filters, key indicators, and other decision-making parameters used for portfolio management. (*Portfolio Management*)

Strategic Goals

The definition of an organization's intended achievements in terms of business and cultural results, within a specified timeframe, and usually associated with specific metrics. (*Portfolio Management*)

Combined Standards Glossary
©2007 Project Management Institute, Four Campus Boulevard, Newtown Square, PA 19073-3299 USA

Strategic Plan

A high-level document that explains the organization's vision and mission, plus the approach that will be adopted to achieve this mission and vision, including the specific goals and objectives to be achieved during the period covered by the document. (*Portfolio Management*)

Strengths, Weaknesses, Opportunities, and Threats (SWOT) Analysis

This information gathering technique examines the project from the perspective of each project's strengths, weaknesses, opportunities, and threats to increase the breadth of the risks considered by risk management. (*PMBOK® Guide* – **Third Edition**)

Style

A set of skills, attributes, or characteristics of a person; the concept refers to a frequent pattern of what is said, done, expressed, or performed by a person demonstrating one's values. It encompasses the modes or patterns of behavior that people exhibit in approaching their work and interacting with others. (*PMCDF*)

Subject-Matter Expert

A person, usually an accomplished performer, who knows the knowledge, performance, and personal competence required for a given Unit or Cluster of Competence. (*PMCDF*)

Subnetwork

A subdivision (fragment) of a project schedule network diagram, usually representing a subproject or a work package. Often used to illustrate or study some potential or proposed schedule condition, such as changes in preferential schedule logic or project scope. (*PMBOK® Guide* – **Third Edition**)

Subphase

A subdivision of a phase. (*PMBOK® Guide* – **Third Edition**)

Subportfolio

A collection of components which includes programs, projects, portfolios, and other work grouped together within a larger portfolio. (*Portfolio Management*)

Subproject

A smaller portion of the overall project created when a project is subdivided into more manageable components or pieces. Subprojects are usually represented in the work breakdown structure. A subproject can be referred to as a project, managed as a project, and acquired from a seller. May be referred to as a subnetwork in a project schedule network diagram. (*PMBOK® Guide* – **Third Edition**)

Successor
SEE   Successor Activity (*PMBOK® Guide* – **Third Edition**)

Successor Activity
The schedule activity that follows a predecessor activity, as determined by their logical relationship. (*PMBOK® Guide* – **Third Edition**)

Summary Activity
A group of related schedule activities aggregated at some summary level, and displayed/reported as a single activity at that summary level. (*PMBOK® Guide* – **Third Edition**)
> SEE ALSO   Subnetwork
> (*PMBOK® Guide* – **Third Edition**)
> Subproject (*PMBOK® Guide* – **Third Edition**)

Sustainment
Activities associated with ensuring that customers continue to receive utility from products. (*Program Management*)

System
An integrated set of regularly interacting or interdependent components created to accomplish a defined objective, with defined and maintained relationships among its components, and the whole producing or operating better than the simple sum of its components. Systems may be either physically process based or management process based, or more commonly a combination of both. Systems for project management are composed of project management processes, techniques, methodologies, and tools operated by the project management team. (*PMBOK® Guide* – **Third Edition**)

Target Completion Date (TC)
An imposed date that constrains or otherwise modifies the schedule network analysis. (*PMBOK® Guide* – **Third Edition**)

Target Finish Date (TF)
The date that work is planned (targeted) to finish on a schedule activity. (*PMBOK® Guide* – **Third Edition**)

Target Schedule
A schedule adopted for comparison purposes during schedule network analysis, which can be different from the baseline schedule. (*PMBOK® Guide* – **Third Edition**)
> SEE ALSO   Baseline (*PMBOK® Guide* – **Third Edition**)

Combined Standards Glossary
©2007 Project Management Institute, Four Campus Boulevard, Newtown Square, PA 19073-3299 USA

Target Start Date (TS)

The date that work is planned (targeted) to start on a schedule activity. (*PMBOK® Guide* – **Third Edition**)

Task

A term for work whose meaning and placement within a structured plan for project work varies by the application area, industry, and brand of project management software. (*PMBOK® Guide* – **Third Edition**)(*PS-WBS*)

Team Members

SEE   Project Team Members (*PMBOK® Guide* – **Third Edition**)

Technical Performance Measurement [Technique]

A performance measurement technique that compares technical accomplishments during project execution to the project management plan's schedule of planned technical achievements. It may use key technical parameters of the product produced by the project as a quality metric. The achieved metric values are part of the work performance information. (*PMBOK® Guide* – **Third Edition**)

Technique

A defined systematic procedure employed by a human resource to perform an activity to produce a product or result or deliver a service, and that may employ one or more tools. (*PMBOK® Guide* – **Third Edition**)(*Program Management*)

Template

A partially complete document in a predefined format that provides a defined structure for collecting, organizing and presenting information and data. Templates are often based upon documents created during prior projects. Templates can reduce the effort needed to perform work and increase the consistency of results. (*PMBOK® Guide* – **Third Edition**)

Threat

A condition or situation unfavorable to the project, a negative set of circumstances, a negative set of events, a risk that will have a negative impact on a project objective if it occurs, or a possibility for negative changes. Contrast with *opportunity.* (*PMBOK® Guide* – **Third Edition**)

Three-Point Estimate [Technique]

An analytical technique that uses three cost or duration estimates to represent the optimistic, most likely, and pessimistic scenarios. This technique is applied to improve the accuracy of the estimates of cost or duration when the underlying activity or cost component is uncertain. (*PMBOK® Guide* – **Third Edition**)

Threshold

A cost, time, quality, technical, or resource value used as a parameter, and which may be included in product specifications. Crossing the threshold should trigger some action, such as generating an exception report. (*PMBOK® Guide* – **Third Edition**)

Tight Matrix

A system in which each project has an assigned work area, and employees sit together in that area while they are working on the project, even though they do not report to the same supervisor. (*Gov't Ext*)

Time and Material (T&M) Contract

A type of contract that is a hybrid contractual arrangement containing aspects of both cost-reimbursable and fixed-price contracts. Time and material contracts resemble cost-reimbursable type arrangements in that they have no definitive end, because the full value of the arrangement is not defined at the time of the award. Thus, time and material contracts can grow in contract value as if they were cost-reimbursable-type arrangements. Conversely, time and material arrangements can also resemble fixed-price arrangements. For example, the unit rates are preset by the buyer and seller, when both parties agree on the rates for the category of senior engineers. (*PMBOK® Guide* – **Third Edition**)

Time-Now Date

SEE   Data Date (DD) (*PMBOK® Guide* – **Third Edition**)

Time-Phase Budget

A project budget that identifies how much money or labor is to be expended on each task for each time period (e.g., month) in the project schedule. (*PS-EVM*)

SEE ALSO Planned Value (PV) (**PS-EVM**)

Time-Sealed Schedule Network Diagram [Tool]

Any project schedule network diagram drawn in such a way that the positioning and length of the schedule activity represents its duration. Essentially, it is a bar chart that includes schedule network logic. (*PMBOK® Guide* – **Third Edition**)

To-Complete Performance Index (TCPI)

The calculated projection of cost performance that must be achieved on remaining work to meet a specified goal, such as the BAC or the

Combined Standards Glossary
©2007 Project Management Institute, Four Campus Boulevard, Newtown Square, PA 19073-3299 USA

management EAC. For example: To-Complete Performance Index = (remaining work) / (budget remaining) = (BAC – EV) / (BAC – AC). (*PS-EVM*)

Tool

Something tangible, such as a template or software program, used in performing an activity to produce a product or result. (***PMBOK® Guide – Third Edition***)(*Program Management*)

Toolbox Meetings

A regular meeting of field supervisors and workers to review important work issues; particularly those pertaining to safety. (***Const Ext***)

Total Float (TF)

The total amount of time that a schedule activity may be delayed from its early start date without delaying the project finish date, or violating a schedule constraint. Calculated using the critical path method technique and determining the difference between the early finish dates and late finish dates. (***PMBOK® Guide – Third Edition***)

> SEE ALSO　Free Float (FF)
> ***PMBOK® Guide – Third Edition***

Total Quality Management (TQM) [Technique]

A common approach to implementing a quality improvement program within an organization. (***PMBOK® Guide – Third Edition***)

Trades

Workers in the various construction disciplines such as carpenters and ironworkers. (***Const Ext***)

Trait

A distinguishing feature of the person's character, usually thought of as a relatively enduring aspect of the person. (***PMCDF***)

Trend Analysis [Technique]

An analytical technique that uses mathematical models to forecast future outcomes based on historical results. It is a method of determining the variance from a baseline of a budget, cost, schedule, or scope parameter by using prior progress reporting periods' data and projecting how much that parameter's variance from baseline might be at some future point in the project if no changes are made in executing the project. (***PMBOK® Guide – Third Edition***)

Triggers

Indications that a risk has occurred or is about to occur. Triggers may be discovered in the risk identification process and watched in the risk

©2007 Project Management Institute, Four Campus Boulevard, Newtown Square, PA 19073-3299 USA

monitoring and control process. Triggers are sometimes called risk symptoms or warning signs. (*PMBOK® Guide* – **Third Edition**)

Triple Constraint

1) A framework for evaluating competing demands. The triple constraint is often depicted as a triangle where one of the sides or one of the corners represent one of the parameters being managed by the project team. (*PMBOK® Guide* – **Third Edition**)

2) A relationship between product scope, time, and cost. If a change is made to any of the three factors, at least one other factor must change. (*Gov't Ext*)

Turn Key

A type of design build project where the design builder does all functions including start up before turning the project over to the owner. (*Const Ext*)

Two-Envelope System

A form of procurement also called "two step" that is performed in two phases. The first phase involves a firm's qualifications. If the firm qualifies the second phase involves pricing. (*Const Ext*)

Unit of Competence

A major segment of overall Competency, typically representing a major function. (*PMCDF*)

Unit Rate Contract

A contract for construction based on established (bid) prices for certain types of work where the final quantities may not be known. (*Const Ext*)

Use It or Lose It

A provision in the annual budget of a government body that requires funds to be spent or obligated by the end of the fiscal year. (*Gov't Ext*)

User

The person or organization that will use the project's product or service. (*PMBOK® Guide* – **Third Edition**)(*PS-WBS*)

> See Also   Customer (*PMBOK® Guide* – **Third Edition**)(*PS-WBS*)

Validation [Technique]

The technique of evaluating a component or product during or at the end of a phase or project to ensure it complies with the specified requirements. Contrast with *verification*. (*PMBOK® Guide* – **Third Edition**)

Value Engineering (VE)

A creative approach used to optimize project life cycle costs, save time, increase profits, improve quality, expand market share, solve problems, and/or use resources more effectively. (*PMBOK® Guide* – **Third Edition**)

Value Management

Value engineering. (*Const Ext*)

Variance

A quantifiable deviation, departure, or divergence away from a known baseline or expected value. (*PMBOK® Guide* – **Third Edition**)

Variance Analysis [Technique]

A method for resolving the total variance in the set of scope, cost, and schedule variables into specific component variances that are associated with defined factors affecting the scope, cost, and schedule variables. (*PMBOK® Guide* – **Third Edition**)

Variance at Completion (VAC)

The difference between the total budget assigned to a project (BAC) and the total cost estimate at completion (EAC). Variance at Completion = Budget at Completion – Estimate at Completion. It represents the amount of expected overrun or underrun. (*PS-EVM*)

Variance Threshold

A predetermined range of normal outcomes that is determined during the planning process and sets the boundaries within which the team practices management by exception. (*PS-EVM*)

Verification [Technique]

The technique of evaluating a component or product at the end of a phase or project to assure or confirm it satisfies the conditions imposed. Contrast with *validation*. (*PMBOK® Guide* – **Third Edition**)

Virtual Team

A group of persons with a shared objective who fulfill their roles with little or no time spent meeting face to face. Various forms of technology are often used to facilitate communication among team members. Virtual teams can be comprised of persons separated by great distances. (*PMBOK® Guide* – **Third Edition**)

Voice of the Customer

A planning technique used to provide products, services, and results that truly reflect customer requirements by translating those customer

Combined Standards Glossary
©2007 Project Management Institute, Four Campus Boulevard, Newtown Square, PA 19073-3299 USA

requirements into the appropriate technical requirements for each phase of project product development. (*PMBOK® Guide* – **Third Edition**)

War Room

1) A room used for project conferences and planning, often displaying charts of cost, schedule status, and other key project data. (*PMBOK® Guide* – **Third Edition**)
2) A room used for project conferences and planning, often displaying maps, charts of cost and schedule status and other key project data. (*Const Ext*)

Weight

A multiplication factor used to convey the relative importance of key criteria used in a scoring model. (*Portfolio Management*)

Weighted Price and Qualifications

SEE   Best Value Selection (*Gov't Ext*)

Work

Sustained physical or mental effort, exertion, or exercise of skill to overcome obstacles and achieve an objective. (*PMBOK® Guide* – **Third Edition**)

Work Authorization [Technique]

A permission and direction, typically written, to begin work on a specific schedule activity or work package or control account. It is a method for sanctioning project work to ensure that the work is done by the identified organization, at the right time, and in the proper sequence. (*PMBOK® Guide* – **Third Edition**)

Work Authorization System [Tool]

A subsystem of the overall project management system. It is a collection of formal documented procedures that defines how project work will be authorized (committed) to ensure that the work is done by the identified organization, at the right time, and in the proper sequence. It includes the steps, documents, tracking system, and defined approval levels needed to issue work authorizations. (*PMBOK® Guide* – **Third Edition**)

Work Breakdown Structure (WBS) [Output/Input]

1) A deliverable-oriented hierarchical decomposition of the work to be executed by the project team to accomplish the project objectives and create the required deliverables. It organizes and defines the total scope of the project. Each descending level represents an increasingly detailed definition of the project work. The WBS is decomposed into work packages. The deliverable orientation of the hierarchy includes both internal and external deliverables. (*PMBOK® Guide* – **Third Edition**)

Combined Standards Glossary
©2007 Project Management Institute, Four Campus Boulevard, Newtown Square, PA 19073-3299 USA

2) A deliverable-oriented grouping of project elements that organizes and defines the total scope of the project. Each descending level represents an increasingly detailed definition of the project work. (*PS-WBS*)(*PS-WBS*)

> SEE ALSO   Contract Work Breakdown Structure (CWBS) (*PMBOK® Guide* – **Third Edition**)
> Control Account (CA) (*PMBOK® Guide* – **Third Edition**)(*PS-WBS*)
> Project Summary Work Breakdown Structure (PSWBS) (*PMBOK® Guide* – **Third Edition**)
> Work Package (*PMBOK® Guide* – **Third Edition**)(*PS-WBS*)

Work Breakdown Structure Component

An entry in the work breakdown structure that can be at any level. (*PMBOK® Guide* – **Third Edition**)(*PS-WBS*)

Work Breakdown Structure Dictionary [Output/Input]

A document that describes each component in the work breakdown structure (WBS). For each WBS component, the WBS dictionary includes a brief definition of the scope or statement of work, defined deliverable(s), a list of associated activities, and a list of milestones. Other information may include: responsible organization, start and end dates, resources required, an estimate of cost, charge number, contract information, quality requirements, and technical references to facilitate performance of the work. (*PMBOK® Guide* – **Third Edition**)(*PS-WBS*)

Work Breakdown Structure Element

Any single work breakdown structure (WBS) element or component and its associated WBS attributes contained within an individual work breakdown structure. (*PS-WBS*)

Work Item

Term no longer in common usage. (*PMBOK® Guide* – **Third Edition**)

> SEE   Activity (*PMBOK® Guide* – **Third Edition**)
> Schedule Activity (*PMBOK® Guide* – **Third Edition**)

Work Package

A deliverable or project work component at the lowest level of each branch of the work breakdown structure. The work package includes the schedule activities and schedule milestones required to complete the

Combined Standards Glossary
©2007 Project Management Institute, Four Campus Boulevard, Newtown Square, PA 19073-3299 USA

work package deliverable or project work component. (*PMBOK® Guide –* **Third Edition**)(*PS-WBS*)

      SEE ALSO   Control Account (CA)
                          (*PMBOK® Guide –* **Third Edition**)

Work Performance Information [Output/Input]

Information and data, on the status of the project schedule activities being performed to accomplish the project work, collected as part of the direct and manage project execution processes. Information includes: status of deliverables; implementation status for change requests, corrective actions, preventive actions, and defect repairs; forecasted estimates to complete; reported percent of work physically completed; achieved value of technical performance measures; start and finish dates of schedule activities. (*PMBOK® Guide –* **Third Edition**)

Workaround [Technique]

A response to a negative risk that has occurred. Distinguished from contingency plan in that a workaround is not planned in advance of the occurrence of the risk event. (*PMBOK® Guide –* **Third Edition**)

Zero-Balance Budgeting

A budget process where each year's budget starts with a zero balance, requiring justification of every expense and income item. (*Gov't Ext*)

      SEE ALSO   Obligation (*Gov't Ext*)

Combined Standards Glossary
©2007 Project Management Institute, Four Campus Boulevard, Newtown Square, PA 19073-3299 USA

REFERENCES

Construction Extension to A Guide to the Project Management Body of Knowledge (PMBOK® Guide) — 2000 Edition. Newtown Square, PA: Project Management Institute, 2003.

Government Extension to A Guide to the PMBOK® Guide Third Edition. Newtown Square, PA: Project Management Institute, 2006.

A Guide to the Project Management Body of Knowledge (PMBOK® Guide). 3rd ed. Newtown Square, PA: Project Management Institute, 2004.

Organizational Project Management Maturity Model (OPM3®). Newtown Square, PA: Project Management Institute, 2003.

Practice Standard for Earned Value Management. Newtown Square, PA: Project Management Institute, 2005.

Practice Standard for Work Breakdown Structures. Newtown Square, PA: Project Management Institute, 2006.

Project Manager Competency Development (PMCD) Framework. Newtown Square, PA: Project Management Institute, 2002.

The Standard for Portfolio Management. Newtown Square, PA: Project Management Institute, 2006.

The Standard for Program Management. Newtown Square, PA: Project Management Institute, 2006.

APPENDIX

The *Combined Standards Glossary* was compiled by Ann C. Davidson, M.L.S., of Davidson Library Services. Staff members of the Project Management Institute who also contributed to the *Combined Standards Glossary* project include:

Information Specialist: Marian Quinn, M.L.S.
   PMI® James R. Snyder Center for Project Management
   Knowledge and Wisdom

Manager, Standards: Donn Greenberg, PMP
   PMI Standards Department

Product Editor: Roberta Storer
   PMI Publications Department

Publications Planner: Barbara Walsh
   PMI Publications Department

©2007 Project Management Institute, Four Campus Boulevard, Newtown Square, PA 19073-3299 USA